SHAKSPERE:

HIS

BIRTHPLACE AND ITS NEIGHBOURHOOD.

BY JOHN R. WISE.

ILLUSTRATED BY W. J. LINTON

Porch of Trinity Church

M.DCCC.LXI.

British Library Cataloguing-in-Publication Data
A catalogue record for this book is available from the
British Library

John Richard de Capel Wise

John Rickard de Capel Wise was born on 1st April 1831, as the eldest son of John Robert Wise (a former British consul-general in Sweden) and his wife Jane. He attended Grantham Grammar School in the market town of Grantham, Lincolnshire, England – and subsequently enrolled at the University of Oxford. He began his studies in 1849, at Lincoln College, but took no degree, and left the university to travel abroad.

On returning to England he wandered through many country districts, frequently changing his residence. Wise held radical views on religion and politics, and according to his friend, Walter Crane (a celebrated artist and illustrator), Wise had been intended for the Church – but left Oxford due to his theological disagreements. Wise also quarrelled with his parents, apparently 'on account of his free opinions.' During the course of his wanderings, he came to know John Chapman, the editor of the *Westminster Review*. As a result of this friendship, for many years he wrote the section on *Belles-Lettres* in that magazine, but withdrew suddenly owing to political differences with Chapman. His relations with the *Westminster* also brought him the acquaintance of George Henry Lewes and George Eliot.

After this, Wise contributed to the *Reader,* a weekly periodical which advanced political views as radical as Wise's own. He was also a correspondent for a London paper during the Franco-Prussian War in 1870. Wise never married, but enjoyed a prolific career in writing. His first work was a pamphlet of poems called *Robin Hood* published in 1855. In 1860 he issued a novel in two volumes called *The Cousin's Courtship* with little success. Following repeated visits to Stratford-upon-Avon he published (1861) a volume on *Shakespeare: his Birthplace and its Neighbourhood*. The book contained a description of the local scenery, the natural history, the literary associations and dialect of Stratford-upon-Avon.

He lived in the New Forest (in southern England) in the early 1860s, which allowed him to research and write his book on the locality, but by the summer of 1863 he was residing in lodgings near Hathersage in the Peak District. This book was *The New Forest: its History and its Scenery* (1862), by far his most popular work, and it contained sixty-two illustrations drawn by Walter Crane and engraved by William James Linton. The most sought after edition by collectors was the 'artist's edition' of 1883, to which Heywood Sumner added twelve etchings, and which had Linton's woodcuts mounted on India paper.

Wise had hoped to write a book on the Peak District, similar to the one he had written for the New Forest but did not receive sufficient encouragement to go on with the work. By 1875 he was settled at Sandsend, but soon after migrated to Edwinstowe, Nottinghamshire. In 1881 he anonymously published an elaborate volume called *The First of May: A Fairy Masque*, which he dedicated to Charles Darwin. It was also illustrated by Walter Crane, but was financially unsuccessful. Wise re-visited Lyndhyrst in the New Forest in August 1889, and stayed there throughout the winter.

" Doubtless Shakspere had seen many a Bottom in the old Warwickshire hamlets ; many
a Sir Nathaniel playing ' Alissander,' and finding himself ' a little o'erparted.' He had
been with Snug the joiner, Quince the carpenter, and Flute the bellows-mender, when a
boy, we will not question, and acted with them, and written their parts for them."

FROUDE's History of England, vol. i. ch. i. pp. 69, 70.

" Shakspere had to be left with his kingcups and clover : pansies—the passing clouds—
the Avon's flow—and the undulating hills and woods of Warwick."

RUSKIN's Modern Painters, vol. iv. ch. xx. § 29, p. 373.

CONTENTS.

CHAP.   PAGE

I. INTRODUCTORY 1

II. STRATFORD-UPON-AVON — THE HOUSE WHERE SHAKSPERE
      WAS BORN 13

III. STRATFORD—THE PARISH CHURCH 20

IV. THE GRAMMAR SCHOOL — CHAPEL OF THE GUILD — NEW
      PLACE 28

V. THE CHAMBERLAIN'S BOOKS, ETC., OF STRATFORD—PRIVATE
      MANUSCRIPTS IN STRATFORD 35

VI. CHARLECOTE PARK 43

VII. WELCOMBE AND SNITTERFIELD 58

VIII. SHOTTERY 70

IX. THE AVON—LUDDINGTON—WELFORD 75

X. "PIPING PEBWORTH—DANCING MARSTON " . . . 86

XI. WARWICKSHIRE ORCHARDS AND HARVEST HOMES . . 93

XII. THE PROVINCIALISMS OF SHAKSPERE 103

XIII. SHAKSPERE 116

GLOSSARY OF WORDS STILL USED IN WARWICKSHIRE TO
    BE FOUND IN SHAKSPERE. 149

INDEX 159

NOTE.

Whilst these sheets were in the press, the munificent bequest of 2,500*l.*, left, together with an annuity of 60*l.*, by the late Mr. John Shakespear, of Worthington, Leicestershire, has been set aside by a decree of the Court of Chancery, and the committee for the repairs of the house in Henley Street, where Shakspere was born, find themselves liable for a heavy debt. Surely, however, the English nation, which loves and reverences its greatest poet, will not suffer the people of Stratford long to need assistance for repairing the birthplace of Shakspere, when Australia, to her honour, is setting up a statue to him in her principal town.

LIST OF ILLUSTRATIONS.

	PAGE
The Tombs in the Chancel—*Frontispiece.*	
Porch of Trinity Church—*Title-page.*	
The room in which Shakspere was born	12
His Father's House in Henley Street	13
Old Font of Trinity Church	19
Trinity Church	20
The Latin School	28
The Mathematical School	34
Back of Grammar School, and Guild Chapel	35
Shakspere's Desk	42
Charlecote Hall	43
Autograph and Seal of Sir Thomas Lucy	57
Stratford, from Welcombe Grounds	58
Welcombe Thorns	69
Anne Hathaway's Cottage	70
Avon at the Weir Brake	75
Bidford Bridge	86
The Foot-Bridge at the Mill	92
At Luddington	93
Apple Gathering	102
The House in Henley Street as Restored	103
Honey Stalks	115
Bust of Shakspere	116
Remains of Shakspere's House at New Place	148
Autograph	158

SHAKSPERE:

BIRTHPLACE AND ITS NEIGHBOURHOOD.

CHAPTER I.

INTRODUCTORY.

How often do we hear it said, "How I should have liked
to have seen Shakspere." Had we seen him, most likely
we should have found him a man like ourselves, greater
because he was not less but more of a man, suffering
terribly from all the ills to which flesh is heir; and we
should have been disappointed and said, "Is this all, is this
what we came out to see?" and proved ourselves in all
probability mere valets to the hero. It is better as it is;
we must be content to let Shakspere have had Ben Jonson
for a friend, and joyfully to take his testimony, brief as
that is,—"I loved the man, and do honour his memory,

1

on this side idolatry, as much as any. He was, indeed, honest, and of an open and free nature."

Though springing from an excellent feeling, it is a mistaken wish to see with the physical eye the world's great men. The least part of a great man is his materia presence. It is better for us each to draw our own ideal of Shakspere; to picture his face so calm and happy and gentle, as his friends declare his spirit to have been; yet not unseared by misfortune and chastened by the divine religion of sorrow. It is better as it is. We know not for certain even his likeness, or his form. The earth-dress falls away, the worthless mortal coil is shuffled off, and only what is pure and noble, the essence of all that is great in the man, remains for evermore as a precious birthright to all the world.

A more reasonable wish is one, also often heard, that we had some diary of Shakspere, some of his private letters to his wife or his children, or even a correspondence with Ben Jonson. I do not know that even this is to be regretted. Ben Jonson's correspondence has been brought to light, and alas! he has been found out to have been a poor government spy. And though of Shakspere we can confidently trust,

That whatever record leap to light,
He never shall be shamed ;

yet I still think it better as it is. The gods should live

by themselves. And as was the case with the physical, so with the spiritual man, it is best for us to draw our own ideal. Of the greatest poets who have ever lived, the world knows nothing. Homer is to us only a name. Of the singer of the *Nibelungen Lied* we know not so much as that. And yet all that is good and noble of them remains to us. We surely will not grudge our Shakspere their happy lot. The truest biographer of Shakspere, it has been well said, is the most earnest student of his plays. Even did we possess the private letters and diaries of Shakspere, what use could we make of them? One man only has been born, since Shakspere died, fit to write his history, and that man, Goethe, is a foreigner. Most biographies, even where the amplest information abounds, are mere catalogues of dates, a history of what the great man eats and drinks, and whatwithal he is clothed.

To know Shakspere's life would undoubtedly be to know one of the highest lives ever lived. To know his struggles, for struggles he had, bitter as ever man endured, his sonnets alone would testify; to trace how from darkness he fought his way to light, how he moulded circumstances, how he bore up against fortune and misfortune, were indeed to know a history such as we cannot expect ever now to have revealed.

Still the wish will ever linger that we did possess some scraps of information. We ever shall care to know what we can about our greatest men ; it is the one feeling that will last to all time : and this love, this reverence for the good and great men of the earth, is amongst the best traits in our human nature. I will not blame even that feeling which hoards up Garrick cups, and mulberry tooth-picks as treasures; even this, in its way, is a testimony to the infinite worth of true greatness. Halliwell and Collier have given up their time in searching every record and deed for the minutest allusion to our poet; and the least thing they have discovered has been eagerly welcomed.

But we seem ever doomed to disappointment; not one scrap, not a half-sheet of paper of Shakspere's handwriting ever turns up : the most painful search adds but little to our knowledge; nothing beyond a name or two, or another date or so. His life is at best but a collection of fines and leases; everything connected with his private life perished with him ; when he died he carried with him his secret. No external history could of course reveal to us the fount of his inspiration: that is just as visible now, as ever, to the seeing eye, and the sympathetic love of any reader. But the man himself, what he did here on earth, how he struggled with outward circumstances, and how from being the apprentice to a butcher or a woolstapler he rose to become the writer of *Hamlet*, we know not. It is idle to say that this is of second-rate importance, and that Shakspere's inner life, which may be gleaned from his writings, is alone worth knowing; men ever will wish to know his exterior life.

I feel that I can add nothing new to the researches of Collier and Halliwell, but I have always thought that something might be written better than the present guide-books to Stratford. Here was Shakspere born, and here he died; here in the archives of the town the only information about him and his family exists; and here, still more important, is the country where he rambled when a boy, and which he loved when a man; and here people still come, day after day, on a pilgrimage to his house, showing that hero-worship is not dead, proving that even in these days the world pays homage to its great men.

The aim of this little book is not very high, but if it will, in some measure, take away the reproach of meagreness from the hand-books to Stratford, and throw some little light on the text of Shakspere, by giving the reader a better idea of the land where the poet lived, I shall be very well content.

To me it has always appeared a most happy circumstance that Shakspere should have been born in

That shire which we the heart of England well may call,

as his fellow-countryman Drayton sings, and that his child-

hood should have fallen amidst such true rural English
scenery; for it is from the storehouse of childhood that in
after years we draw so much wealth.   Happy indeed was
it that his home should have been amongst the orchards
and woodlands round Stratford, and the meadows of the
Avon.   The perfection of quiet English scenery is it, such
as he himself has drawn in the *Midsummer Night's Dream*,
and *The Winter's Tale*, and *As You Like It*, and a hundred
places.   I cannot but hold the theory of the effects of local
causes on a poet's mind, remembering what the poets
themselves have said.   Coleridge declared that the memo-
ries of his youth were so graven on his mind, that when a
man and far away from the spot, he could still see the
river Otter flowing close to him, and hear its ripple as
plainly as when in years long past he wandered by its side;
and Jean Paul Richter, when lamenting how greatly the
absence of the sea had affected his writings, exclaimed,
" I die without ever having seen the ocean; but the ocean
of eternity I shall not fail to see."   And just as climate
modifies the physical condition of a nation, so scenery
affects the mental condition of a poet.   I have no wish to
strain the theory.   I know well that a truth may be so
overstated that it at last becomes a falsehood; I know
too that a poet's mind cannot be tied down to any spot, but
it takes a colour from everything which it sees, and that

the saying of Thucydides, ἀνδρῶν ἐπιφανῶν πᾶσα γη τάφος, will bear reversing, and all the earth is as truly the birth-place of a great man as his grave; yet still I somehow think that the quiet fields round Stratford, and the gentle flow of the Avon, so impressed themselves upon Shakspere's mind, that his nature partook of their gentleness and quietness.

Take up what play you will, and you will find glimpses there of the scenery round Stratford. His maidens ever sing of " blue-veined violets," and " daisies pied," and " pansies that are for thoughts," and " ladies'-smocks all silver-white," that still stud the meadows of the Avon. You catch pictures of the willows that grow ascaunt the brooks, showing the under-part of their leaves, so white and hoar, in the stream ; * and of orchards, too, when

The moon tips with silver all the fruit-tree tops.

I do not think it is any exaggeration to say that nowhere in England are meadows so full of beauty as those round Stratford. I have seen them by the river-side in early

* Virgil, who, with all his shortcomings and failings, had a real love for Nature, and, as long as he kept to descriptions of her, was always truthful, describes the willow somewhat similarly,—" glaucâ canentia fronde salicta " (*Georgic* ii. 13), though it is a very inferior picture to Shakspere's of the leaves reflected in the water. Virgil was probably thinking of the willow-leaves when the wind stirred them, making them glisten with silver.

spring burnished with gold; and then later, a little before hay-harvest, chased with orchisses, and blue and white milkwort, and yellow rattle-grass, and tall moon-daisies: and I know nowhere woodlands so sweet as those round Stratford, filled with the soft green light made by the budding leaves, and paved with the golden ore of primroses, and their banks veined with violets.* All this,

---

* The finest part of Drayton's *Polyolbion* is the thirteenth book, where he describes the scenery of his native Warwickshire, and of his "old Arden." The following passage will interest the reader, as a description of the country in Shakspere's time, Drayton being born only one year before Shakspere:—

> Brave Warwick that abroad so long advanced her Bear,
> By her illustrious Earls renowned everywhere:
> Above her neighbouring shires which always bore her head,
> My native country, then, which so brave spirits hast bred,
> If there be virtues yet remaining in thy earth,
> Or any good of thine thou bredst into my birth,
> Accept it as thine own, whilst now I sing of thee,
> Of all thy later brood the unworthiest though I be.
>
> .   .   .   .
>
> .   .   .   .
>
> When Phœbus lifts his head out of the watery wave,
> No sooner doth the earth her flowery bosom brave,
> At such time as the year brings on the pleasant spring,
> But Hunt's up to the morn, the feathered sylvans sing;
> And, in the lower grove, as on the rising knoll,
> Upon the highest spray of every mounting pole,
> There quiresters are perched, with many a speckled breast:
> Then from her burnished gates the goodly glittering East

and the tenderness that such beauty gives, you find in the pages of Shakspere; and it is not too much to say that he painted them, because they were ever associated in his mind with all that he held precious and dear, both of the earliest and the latest scenes of his life.

Therefore I repeat, that it was well that Shakspere was born here. And I dwell especially upon his love for flowers,—a love always manifested by our great poets:

> Gilds every mountain top, which late the humorous night
> Bespangled had with pearl, to please the morning's sight;
> On which, the mirthful quires, with their clear open throats
> Unto the joyful morn so strain their warbling notes,
> That hills and valleys ring, and e'en the echoing air
> Seems all composed of sounds about them everywhere.
> The throstle with shrill sharps, as purposely he sung
> To awake the listless sun, or chiding that so long
> He was in coming forth that should the thickets thrill;
> The woosel near at hand, that hath a golden bill,
> As nature him had marked, of purpose t' let us see
> That from all other birds his tunes should different be:
> For with their vocal sounds they sing to pleasant May;
> Upon his dulcet pipe the merle doth only play.
> When, in the lower brake, the nightingale hard by,
> In such lamenting strains the joyful hours doth ply,
> As though the other birds she to her tunes would draw.

But the passage does but faint justice to the sweetness of the birds in the Warwickshire woodlands. The reader will remember how, in the *Midsummer Night's Dream*, Shakspere sings of the nightingale, and the " woosel-cock with his orange tawny bill," and " the throstle with his note so true; " and they may still all be heard singing as sweetly as ever in the woods around Stratford.

by Spenser, and Chaucer, and Milton, who seem to regard them with a human sympathy, and to endow them, too, with human feelings. So Shakspere loved, as Lord Herbert of Cherbury would have said, " our fellow-creatures the plants; " and so speak Imogen and Perdita of them, and so, too, Ophelia. Violets Ophelia would have given to her brother; but they died all, when her father died. And I dwell also upon this love for flowers, because we must remember that God has given them, as it were, as a peculiar gift to the poor (that is, to the great body of mankind), for their delight and their contemplation. Other things they have not—pictures, nor gardens, nor libraries, nor sculpture-galleries; but flowers they always have, and it is the contemplation and the love of them that distinguishes us from the beasts of the field.*

Happy, indeed, therefore, was Shakspere's lot to have been born in the country among such scenes! far happier

---

* It is true that Shakspere can paint sea-cliffs, as in *Lear*; or mountains, as in *Cymbeline*; or the sea in a storm, as in the *Tempest*; but he never dwells upon them with that fondness with which he paints his own lowland meadows. This must certainly, in a great measure, be attributed to the reasons given in the text, but partly also to the fact, that man in Shakspere's day had not yet learnt to see a beauty in the clouds, or the wild ravine, or the stormy sea. For this insight we must thank our modern poets and painters; though we must ever remember that there are touches and lines in Shakspere describing mountains and storm, and sunset scenes and clouds, which have never been equalled.

than befell his great fellow-poets, Spenser and Milton, both born in the turmoil of London. And surely, too, it was well that he was born amongst country rustics, and that from the scenes of early life he was able to gather strength, and to idealize, without weakening their reality, his Christopher Slys, his Quinces the carpenters, and his Snugs the joiners, such as we may easily conceive he saw and knew in his boyhood.

I know that it is often brought as a reproach against him that he should have drawn them; but I, for my own part, find in this Shakspere's greatest merit, feeling assured that there is nothing insignificant in humanity, and that the humblest man is by no means the worthless thing generally thought. Surely I think, that in painting these rough forms so lovingly, we may detect Shakspere's true greatness of mind. And the simple thought that nature has made the most numerous of the world's family these same so-called common men, might inspire us with a wish to know and to love them. By painting them, Shakspere could better paint the complexities and troubles of daily life, with its hard toil, such as will last as long as the world lasts. These things may be in themselves very paltry, but they cease to be paltry when we know that by them millions of human beings are strangely affected.

And here let me take the opportunity of saying, what

has been often said before, but which cannot be too often
repeated, that Shakspere's chief excellence lies in this, that
he has not drawn mere lay-figures, but human, breathing,
complex men and women—not Romans, not Greeks, but
simply men; that he has never obtruded mere party
creeds, but given us true religion; never painted mere
finite systems, but true perennial human sympathy; and
that he has never forgotten the broad principle, that
whether Saxon or Celt, Jew or Gentile, we are all bro-
thers; that, in fact, to use his own words, he has ever
"held the mirror up to nature," reflecting there all forms
and shapes, but reflecting them with the charity that looks
upon a brother's shortcomings in pity, knowing well how
utterly impossible it is to judge another.

The Room in which he was Born

The House in Henley Street.

CHAPTER II.

STRATFORD-UPON-AVON—THE HOUSE WHERE
SHAKSPERE WAS BORN.

THIS little country town lies in the Vale of the Red Horse,
so called from the giant figure of a horse cut in the red
marl on the side of the Edgehills, some twelve miles off,
and which gives its name, like its fellow on the Berkshire
hills, to the surrounding country. The Avon, after passing

under the walls of Warwick Castle, and through the park
of Charlecote, widens out broader and shallower as it
approaches the town, where used to be a ford, still visible
by the side of the bridge, from which the place takes its
name, the Saxon prefix of " Strǣte " or " Stret " signifying
a street.

It is, like most of our English country towns, very quiet
all the week, but waking into some little stir on market-
days and fairs. There is nothing about it to attract atten-
tion; no old gates, no picturesque old buildings, as at the
neighbouring city of Warwick ; nothing but the Avon,
and the surrounding country, and the one name of Shakspere. And, since the traveller will only take an interest
in it as connected with Shakspere, I shall not go into the
history of the place, but leave that to the local historian,
and confine myself entirely to what relates to Shakspere.

The first spot which every one looks for is Shakspere's
birthplace. It stands in Henley Street; and though there
is no absolute evidence that he was born there, yet we
know that his father rented it in 1552, and this, coupled
with the tradition, makes the fact nearly certain. The
property was subsequently purchased by his father for
forty pounds in 1575 ; and from the fine levied at the time
we learn that it consisted of two messuages, and two
gardens, and two orchards. In 1597 his father sold a

small portion of the land for two pounds, and in the deed relating to the sale we find him described as a yeoman.*

The house has passed through many changes ; but recently, thanks to the liberality of the late Mr. John Shakspere, and to the good taste of the people of Stratford, it has been restored to its original state in Shakspere's time, and been separated from the surrounding buildings, and the garden planted with all the flowers the poet sings of so lovingly in his plays. The house is one of the old timbered houses that may still be seen standing in many parts of the county, with their great beams chequering the walls with squares, and their high-pitched gable roofs and dormer windows.

Come, we will go in and see the room where was born the man in whose pages live all the poetry, and nobleness, and worth of one of the best ages of English history. It is but a platitude to say that this room stands before all palaces. And as we look at it, and remember that pro- bably it was much scantier and smaller, we bethink our- selves how little Nature cares for her greatest children. She flings them by in obscure corners of the world, leaving them to fight their way. In poverty have been born the world's greatest men. Homer was born, no one knows

---

* Mr. Halliwell, in his accurate *Life of Shakspere*, gives both the fine and this document in full, pp. 34, 37.

where; Socrates was the son of a midwife; and Newton's and Burns's birthplaces were ploughmen's cottages. So it has been, and so it will be. The order of the world was changed by One born in a manger, and the highest Gospel was preached by fishermen; and States were overthrown by a poor priest, preaching only out of the sincerity of his heart.

Let us note, too, all the signatures on the walls, and not be angry with them, for they are but the expression of a true feeling of love and reverence. It is something to think of, that here to this room should be drawn all men, high and low, rich and poor, to pay homage to the son of a yeoman, or, at most, a mere woolstapler. While such an influence lasts, the world is on the right road. Princes and conquerors, blustering and bullying, pass away; but the works of one genuine man are eternal.

It would be well if for one moment we could see the old Stratford of the sixteenth century; for unless we can throw ourselves back into the past, and into its spirit, even Shakspere is meaningless. The street in which he was born was still, as now, called Henley Street; and consisted, nearer the main town, of old, timbered, high-gabled houses, squared with black oak beams; but towards the other end, where now runs Clopton Lane, was unenclosed land. In the High Street stood the houses of the gentry and the richer tradesmen, with their open courts and galleries, and their rush-strewn floors, and their wide barge-boards, rich with carving. And the Falcon still stood where it does now, as a hostelry, with its red lattices. And opposite to it was " the Great House" of the Cloptons, some day to be the New Place of Shakspere, and the Chapel of the Guild, and the Grammar School, with its staircase outside, and the Guild Hall beneath it, where the companies of players used to perform when the Corporation gave an entertainment ; * and somewhat lower down, below the timbered almshouses, stood the house of the priests of the Guild, with its round dove-tower; and you might just catch a glimpse of the Church of the Trinity,

---

* No doubt these entertainments acted strongly upon the mind of Shakspere when a boy, and perhaps gave him his first bias to the stage. The following extracts from the Chamberlain's books at Stratford, will interest the reader, as showing how frequently the players exhibited. The two companies first mentioned performed when Shakspere's father was bailiff.

1569. Item, payd to the Quene's pleyers . . . ix*li*.

Item, to the Erle of Worcester's pleers . . xij*d*.

1573. Paid to Mr. Bayly for the Earle of Leecester's players vs. viij*d*.

1576. Geven my Lord of Warwicke players . . xvij*s*.

Paid the Earle of Worceter players . . vs. viij*d*.

1577. Paid to my lord of Leyster players . . . xvs.

Paid to my lord of Wosters players . . iij*s*. iiij*d*.

1579. Paid to the Countys of Essex plears . . xiiij*s*. vj*d*.

1580. Paid to the Earle of Darbye's players . . viij*s*. iiij*j*.

1581. Paid the Earle of Worcester his players . . iij*s*. iiij*j*.

Paid to the L. Bartlett his players . . iij*s*. ij*d*.

2

with its timbered and lead-coated spire; and the crosses
still stood here and there in the streets.* And the gallants
moved about the old town in their rich picturesque dresses,
their doublets of velvet, and their slashed shoes, and their
ruffles, and their peach-coloured hose. Trade was then
prospering. The middle-classes of England were for the
first time growing into importance, and the lower classes
were far better off than they had ever before been. And,
going on to more important matters, let us remember that
now was the day-spring of Protestantism, and that the
minds of men were awakening from the deathlike sleep
that had bound them. The spirit of the Reformation
could not end where it began, but passed through everything, altering the whole tendency of English thought.
Learning and philosophical inquiry now marked a new
birthday from which men should date. And the poet is
ever the reflex of all that is noble and good of his time.
His birth becomes a necessity. For every age must have

---

* Two certainly, one in Rother Street and the other at the market cross.
See Wheler's *History of Stratford*, p. 109, from which, together with the
late Captain Saunders' valuable collection of sketches, I have partly drawn
this description of old Stratford. I ought to mention that the existence of
the Falcon rests only upon tradition. The three inns in Shakspere's time,
"The Crowne," "The Beare," and "The Swanne," were all in Bridge
Street, as may be seen in an order of the Corporation, dated 18 Dec.,
8 James I. Probably it was one of the ale-houses, of which there were
thirty within the borough.

its own poet. And just as spinning-machines were the necessity of the eighteenth, so was Shakspere the inevitable outcome of the sixteenth century. The energy of that age must be revealed, not alone in defeating Spanish Armadas or in Reformations, but in some æsthetic shape. And in the drama Shakspere luckily found ready made to hand the materials on which he so impressed the patriotism and the high feeling of his day that they will live to all time. If we do not understand this, we do not understand Shakspere.

Old Font of Trinity Church

Trinity Church, Stratford

CHAPTER III.

STRATFORD—THE PARISH CHURCH.

Renowned Spenser! lie a thought more nigh
To learned Chaucer, and, rare Beaumont! lie
A little nearer Spenser, to make room
For Shakspere, in your threefold, fourfold, tomb.

THE next spot to which we instinctively turn, after the birthplace of Shakspere, is the parish church of Stratford. Very beautiful is it, with its avenue of limes and its great

elms by the river-side, their topmost boughs now red in
the April sun, and the rooks cawing and building in the
branches, and the Avon flowing close by, with the sound
of its splashing weir. It is a spot where any poet might
wish to be buried. And Shakspere lies in the chancel
close to the river, where, if any sounds reach the dead,
he might hear the noise of its weir. It is pleasant to
think of him resting here side by side with his wife, and
his favourite daughter and her husband. It never makes
me sad to look at their graves. His was a lot which
any one might envy—to be laid with those in death whom
they loved dearest in life. And those lines on his grave-
stone—

> Good frend, for Jesus' sake, forbeare
> To digg the dust encloased heare;
> Blest be the man that spares thes stones,
> And curst be he that moves my bones;

which have for so long passed as unmeaning doggrel, are
to me inexpressibly beautiful. I do not for one moment
suppose that Shakspere wrote them; but I do think that
whoever wrote and placed them there, felt he was express-
ing, to the best of his powers, Shakspere's own feelings
on the subject. They are in accordance with all we know
of the man—a simple prayer to be left alone in peace
where some day the dust of all that he best loved would

be laid with him.   It is the same entreaty that his fellow
poet, Spenser, utters in the *Fairy Queen*—

> O dearest God ! me grant, I dead be not defouled.
>
> B. I., Canto x. 42.

And as I before noticed how much happier than Milton's
and Spenser's was Shakspere's lot to be born in the
country, so, too, do I think it far happier for him to be
buried in the quiet church of Stratford than, like them,
in the bustle and roar of London.   No poet, perhaps,
rests so happily as Shakspere.   This is better than being
buried in Westminster Abbey or St. Paul's, to lie at
peace amongst your own.   Goethe rests beside a royal
duke and Schiller ; but I think Shakspere's a far happier
lot.   Dante sleeps in a marble tomb far away from his
native Florence, " *parvi mater amoris*," as he bitterly said ;
but Shakspere rests here under the plain gravestones,
amongst his own friends and kindred.

Let us mark also some of the other inscriptions, parti-
cularly that to Shakspere's favourite daughter Susanna,
the wife of Dr. Hall :—

> Witty above her sexe ; but that's not all—
> Wise to salvation was good Mistris Hall;
> Something of Shakspere was in that, but this
> Wholly of Him with whom she now's in bliss.

It is not too much to conjecture that this gentleness

and goodness of spirit made her Shakspere's favourite daughter. And it is pleasant to know that she placed the inscription to the memory of her mother, who lies on her husband's right hand, and to know, further, that they both earnestly desired to be buried with Shakspere.*

But it always makes me sad, as I read the date on the monument on the wall, to think that almost in the prime of life the poet was snatched away, and what *Hamlets* and *Lears* the world has missed. I hope the old tradition is true, that the last play he wrote was the *Tempest*, with its creations " on the skirts of human nature dwelling." Above all others this play is built upon the firm foundations of spirit, and derives a tragic interest from the fact that the poet himself was so soon to be called away to that spirit-land. Nor let us forget the bust, with its face looking so calm and quiet ; and though perhaps it does not realize Shakspere's countenance to us, still there is about it a certain quietness and gentleness that accords with all that we know of him. " Here is a man who has struggled toughly," I always think of Shakspere, as Goethe said of himself; and the smooth, un-meaning portraits we have of him, give me not the

---

* From a letter written in 1693, from Mr. Dowdall to Mr. Edward Southwell, and published under the title of *Traditionary Anecdotes of Shakspere*, London, 1838.

slightest idea of the man. The bust, however, was sculptured by Gerard Johnson, one of the best artists of his day, and erected only seven years after Shakspere's death, when his features would still be well remembered; and we must therefore regard it as the only authentic likeness of him we possess. Originally it was coloured, the eyes being a light hazel, and the hair and beard auburn. In 1743 it was repainted, and the old colours were faithfully preserved; but in 1793 Malone caused the whole bust to be whitewashed by some common house-painter, for which he righteously suffered the penalty of the well-known epigram.*

The old parish register is full of entries of baptisms and deaths in the Shakspere family, the most important, of course, being—"Baptisms, 1564, April 26. Gulielmus filius Johannis Shakspere;" and yet if you ask where is the font where the three-day-born baby was baptized, it cannot be shown. When I lived near Stratford, the old font was in the possession of a private individual. I trust it may be restored to its proper place. For if there is any one of whom Protestantism may be proud,

* Stranger, to whom this monument is shown,
  Invoke the poet's curses on Malone:
  Whose meddling zeal his barbarous taste displays,
  And daubs his tombstone as he marred his plays.

it is Shakspere ; and surely the font where he was sealed
a member of the Church, and for which, too, in after
life he proved himself a faithful soldier, should not be
allowed to rot to pieces. Milton has in these days been
discovered to be a Unitarian. But against Shakspere the
strictest orthodoxy has never brought a single charge.
Yet if ever there was a man who questioned fate, who
fought "the cruel battle within," and yet remained faithful,
it was Shakspere. Never in any of his plays is there the
slightest symptom of that disbelief which ends in despair
and mockery. Too large-minded for any one particular
creed or system, he ever treats not only religion, but
all things, with the purest spirit of reverence ; and I
do say that he deserves better of his Church than that
the font at which he was baptized should be cast aside
and forgotten.

There is a monument on the north side of the great
east window worth looking at, on account of its connection
with Shakspere, and executed by the same sculptor as his
own, to the memory of John Combe. He was, as is
well known, a money-lender, and the story runs that he
asked Shakspere to write his epitaph, the severity of
which the miser is said never to have forgiven. But
the same thought may be found in different shapes in
literature long before Shakspere's time, and there is pro-

bably but little truth in the tradition, as we find John Combe leaving by his will five pounds to Shakspere.*

The church itself is very beautiful, especially when seen as I have often seen it by night, the moon lighting up the yellow-gray tower, etching its great black shadow on the churchyard, and breaking in soft silver lights upon the clerestory windows. Very beautiful, too, must that chancel have been where Shakspere lies, when the windows were glazed with the forms of saints and angels, and the old oak roof hung down with its pendant figures and carved statues. But all this sinks into utter insignificance when compared with the one fact that this is the church where Shakspere knelt and prayed, and where he confessed the heavy burden and the mystery of the world. I scarcely ever like to put much faith in tradition, but I think we may trust the tradition of Shakspere's deeply religious cast of thought towards the end of his life. I see no reason for disbelieving it. We may surely better accept this than the other vile stories we unhesitatingly swallow. This much I know, gathered from some little experience, that generally speaking, all bad traditions are false, but

---

* The common version is that given by Aubrey:—

    Ten in the hundred lies here ingraved;
    'Tis a hundred to ten his soul is not saved;
    If any man ask who lies in this tomb?
    Oh! oh! quoth the Devil, 'tis my John a Combe.

that good traditions ever contain some germ of truth; the reason being that human nature is too prone to invent not good, but evil report. And through all Shakspere's plays, as I before said, there ever shines forth a reverence not only for religion, but for the mysteries of life and the world. We do ourselves no good by disbelieving this account, testified, as I surely think it is, by the evidence of the sonnets. And in conclusion I would intreat the reader to ponder over this, one of the most beautiful of Shakspere's autobiographical poems:—

> Poor soul, the centre of my sinful earth,
>> Fooled by those rebel powers that thee array,
> Why dost thou pine within, and suffer dearth,
>> Painting thy outward walls so costly gay?
> Why so large cost, having so short a lease,
>> Dost thou upon thy fading mansion spend?
> Shall worms, inheritors of this excess,
>> Eat up thy charge? Is this thy body's end?
> Then, soul, live thou upon thy servant's loss,
>> And let that pine to aggravate thy store:
> Buy terms divine in selling hours of dross:
>> Within be fed, without be rich no more:
> So shalt thou feed on death, that feeds on men,
> And death once dead, there's no more dying then.
>
> *Sonnet* 146.

The Grammar School.

CHAPTER IV.

THE GRAMMAR SCHOOL—CHAPEL OF THE GUILD—
NEW PLACE.

NOT far from the church stood the College of Stratford, whose tithes Shakspere rented, and where John Combe lived, but which has long since been pulled down. The Grammar School, however, where competent authorities say Shakspere must have been educated, still remains.

It is a long, low building, in the main street, with the school-rooms on the upper story, very much altered from its original state in Shakspere's time, one of those good old grammar schools that have done so much good for England. Twenty years ago the old stone staircase, roofed over with tile, by which the boys, from the time of Shakspere, had ascended to the school-room, was standing. But this, too, is gone. Here it was, then, that Shakspere was educated; and in proof of the fact, a desk is shown at which he sat; but we will not inquire too closely into the matter. *Credimus quia incredibile est* must be, in the case of the desk, the ground for our belief. Ben Jonson tells us that Shakspere knew "little Latin and less Greek;" most probably, like all of us, whatever is most valuable, he taught himself. Though I, for my part, should be very well content if our grammar schools, and all other schools and colleges, would teach but " little Latin and less Greek," and more German and French. Underneath the school-room is the former Hall of the Stratford Guild, where, probably, Shakspere learnt more than in the room above, for there, as was said in a previous chapter, the various companies of players performed before the corporation.

Adjoining the grammar school is the Chapel of the Guild, which appears, from an entry in the Corporation

Books, in February, 159$\frac{4}{5}$, to have been temporarily used
as the school, and the commentators bring forward the
passage in *Twelfth Night* (act iii. scene 2), where Malvolio is described wearing "yellow stockings, and cross-
gartered, like a pedant that keeps a school i' the church,"
as an allusion to the circumstance, which probably is only
accidental, as there used to be school-rooms in many of
the old churches, as to this day in the Priory Church
at Christchurch, in Hampshire. In the chapel there was
a pew belonging to New Place, and here in Shakspere's
time the walls were frescoed with paintings, which were
whitewashed over by the Puritans, and have since fallen to
pieces.*

One spot was there which we should all have loved
more than any other—New Place, where Shakspere passed
his last days. A clergyman of the name of Gastrell, into
whose possession it eventually came, annoyed by visitors
and inquiries, not only cut down the very mulberry-
tree Shakspere planted, but to save the taxes, razed the
house itself. I trust he lived to repent of his deed,

---

* In Wheler's *History of Stratford*, pp. 98, 99, 100, will be found an
account of some of these paintings. Leland, in his *Itinerary*, says, "Aboute
the body of this chaple was curiously paynted the Daunce of Death, commonly called the Daunce of Powles, because the same was sometime there
paynted about the cloysters on the north-west syde of Powles Church,
pulled down by the Duke of Somerset tempore E. 6."

and that he some day read how a heathen king, when he destroyed Thebes, spared the home of its poet. The old house, says Dugdale, in his *History of Warwickshire,* was built by Sir Hugh Clopton, Knt., in Henry VII.'s reign, " a fair house, made of brick and timber," and in Sir Hugh's will was called " the Great House." In 1563 it passed by sale out of the Clopton family, and was purchased in 1597 by Shakspere, who entirely repaired and remodelled it, changing the name to New Place. The fact of his purchasing the best house in Stratford when still young, proves how soon he rose to prosperity. Here, too, at the outbreak of the civil war, Henrietta Maria kept her court for three weeks. A modern house is built on the old site, but in a part of what was Shakspere's garden, with happy propriety, stands the Stratford Theatre. To myself there has always seemed something very beautiful in Shakspere's coming back to his native town to spend the rest of his days among his friends and kindred. He was contented and happy with his lot, and this "measureless content" is ever the mark of true greatness. And in that town where he was born he was content to die. And fate ordained, as in Raphael's case, that that day which saw his birth was alone worthy to see his death.

As was before said, all the relics of former days have

passed away from Stratford. The College and New **Place**
are both gone; and the house in Chapel Lane, sold by
Getley to Shakspere, has been destroyed. There are not
even any picturesque old houses, that so link us with the
past, still standing; one only in the High Street, with its
carved barge-boards and its ornamented corbels under the
windows, bearing the date of 1596. But the whole town,
though, is interesting when connected with Shakspere.

Fairer seems the ancient city, and the sunshine seems more fair,
That he once has trod its pavement, that he once has breathed its air.

The very streets speak to us of him. In *Timon of Athens*
(act iv. scene 3) occur the following lines:—

It is the pasture lards the brother's sides,
The want that makes him lean;

the meaning of which was a complete riddle to all commentators. The late Mr. Singer very happily proposed
"rother's sides," that is, oxen's, obviously the true reading.
And in Stratford to this day is there a street still called
Rother Street, and formerly the Rother Market, that is,
the market for cattle, which is still held there.* Again,

* To those who are interested in word-lore, the following note may, perhaps, be acceptable, about a word still used in Warwickshire, but about
which so little is known in the dictionaries. *Rother* is said by Golding to
mean black cattle, but probably any sort, as it is derived from the Saxon,
hryther, a quadruped, connected with *rout* or *rawt*, to bellow or low like an

there is Sheep Street, which is invariably pronounced Ship Street by the lower orders. And this pronunciation we find in Shakspere. Thus, in the *Comedy of Errors* (act iv. scene 1), Antipholus of Ephesus says to Dromio of Syracuse—

> How now, a madman ? Why, thou peevish *sheep*,
> What *ship* of Epidamnus stays for me?

Again, in *The Two Gentlemen of Verona* (act i. scene 1), Speed thus laments :—

> Twenty to one he is *shipped* already,
> And I have played the *sheep* in losing him.

And Shakspere in one of his poems actually rhymes the word " sheep " as if it were spelled " ship."

But leaving these minor considerations, let us look steadily at the one fact, how a truly noble man can

---

ox; as βοῦς, from βοάω. We meet with the word in a petition of Parliament from Wotton Basset to Charles I., about " the free common of pasture for the feeding of all manner of rother-beasts, as cowes." Again, in the parish register of Harbing, Sussex, is an account of " a well-disposed person who gave a cow to the inhabitants on their keeping in order a bridge called Rother Bridge." And in Worcestershire and Warwickshire, the manure of cattle is still called " rother-soil." The village of Rotherwell, near Horncastle, where the petition to Henry VIII. was drawn up in 1536, and Rotherfield, a hamlet in Sussex, and the towns of Rotheram and Rotherhithe, I may notice. are derived from this word; *hithe*, in the last compound, signifying a wharf.

3

ennoble even material things; can make the very stones
of the street and the very walls of the houses full of
romance. It is equally true in another sense than that in
which it was written—

> Outward forms receive
> Their finer influences from the life within.

And so the mere name of Shakspere consecrates the old
town for ever, and fills it with beauty. And he himself,
though long dead, still speaks, and still continues to shed
an influence incalculable to all ends of the earth, through
all time.

The Mathematical School

Back of Grammar School, and Guild Chapel

CHAPTER V.

THE CHAMBERLAIN'S BOOKS, ETC. OF STRATFORD.—
PRIVATE MANUSCRIPTS IN STRATFORD.

VERY interesting are the Chamberlain's accounts of Stratford, for they give us all the reliable information, brief as
it is, that we possess of Shakspere's family, and as the
reader is not likely to inspect them, I have determined to
give a short summary of their contents.* They enable us

---

* I here take the opportunity of thanking Mr. W. O. Hunt for his
repeated kindnesses in allowing me to inspect the corporation books, &c. of

to see the varying circumstances of Shakspere's father, and
prove, apart from all other considerations, that Shakspere
might have been driven by sheer necessity and poverty to
seek his fortune. The first entry that I shall quote is
dated January 10, 156¾, when his father was one of the
Chamberlains of Stratford.

"Item, payd to Shakspeyr for a pec tymbur   .   iijs."
We must, of course, bear in mind that the value of money
was nearly three times as much as it is now.   And in a
meeting of a hall, held January 26 in the same year, we
find :—

"Item, at the same hall the chambur ys
        found in arrerage and ys in det
        unto John Shakspeyre .   .   .   xxvs. viijd."
Proving not only that Shakspere's father was not in want
of money, but was a man of some substance.   I am not, of
course, one of those who care in the least, or think it of
the slightest value, to prove that Shakspere, or his father,
was "a gentleman born," as the clown in the *Winter's Tale*
would say.   But I think that this information is important
when taken in connection with what follows.   Again, in
1565, we find :—

Stratford, and in giving me any information he was able. The way in which
they are kept and preserved might be profitably imitated by other corpora-
tions, who seem often not at all aware of the valuable historical matter to be
found in their documents.

"Item, payd to Shakspeyr for a rest of
    old det   .   .   .   .   . iij*l.* ij*s.* vij*d.*"

"In this accompt the chambur ys in
    det unto John Shakspeyr to be
    payd unto hym by the next cham-
    berlens   .   .   .   .   . vij*s.* iiij*d.*"

All tending to prove that John Shakspere was a man
who could afford to let his money lie by. But his social
position in the town is still more distinctively shown by
a list dated the 30th of August, 1564, where we find
only one burgess giving more than he does for the relief
of the poor, who were suffering in that year from the
plague.* Another meeting is held on the 6th and the
27th of September; and again on the 20th of October,
when he gave in a similar proportion. All things seem
prospering with him. In 1569, he is the chief magis-
trate of Stratford. In 1570, he rents Ingon Meadow
Farm. In 1575, he buys the property in Henley
Street. The tide of fortune then suddenly turns. Three
years afterwards, we find in the corporation books that
he, with another alderman, is excepted from paying the

---

* Mr. Halliwell, in his *Life of Shakspere*, gives this and other documents
in full from the Chamberlain's books, &c. at Stratford, leaving me nothing
new to add, and to the extreme accuracy of his extracts I beg to testify,
having compared them with the originals.

full levy of six and eightpence for equipping " three
pikemen, two bellmen, and an archer," showing that from
a prosperous man he was fast declining. Again, later in
the same year, the state of his affairs is more significantly
shown by the fact that, in an order for the relief of the
poor, he is excused from any payment. And in the March
of the following year, his name is marked as a defaulter for
three and threepence, the reduced sum which was levied
on him for purchasing the armour.

From other sources we know his altered position. In
1578, he is obliged to mortgage for forty pounds his estate of
Ashbies, near Wilmecote, which he received with his wife;
and in 1579, he sold the interest of his property at Snitterfield
for four pounds. All things are evidently going wrong.

Returning, however, to the corporation books, we find the
following remarkable entry, dated September 6, 1586 :—

" At thys halle William Smythe and Richard Courte
are chosen to be aldermen in the places of John Wheler
and John Shaxspere; for that Mr. Wheler dothe desyre
to be put owt of the companye, and Mr. Shaxspere doth
not come to the halles when they be warned, nor hathe not
done of longe tyme."

He is removed; and we meet his name but once or
twice more. But in a return procured by Sir Thomas
Lucy we find him in 1592, mentioned amongst other

recusants as staying away from church, for fear of being
arrested for debt. To this has the prosperous man been
reduced. It is a sad history. Then suddenly comes the
wonderful change. In 1596, we find the man, who was
almost beggared but four years before, applying to the
herald's office for a grant of arms. There can, I think, be
but one solution, that the son was now prospering and
helped him. And this is corroborated by the fact that we
know that in the following year the poet bought New
Place. A few more years pass by, and, in 1601, John
Shakspere dies, having lived to see the success of his son.
It is, indeed, a strange eventful history. And I have told
the story in its barest shape, without conjecture or remark,
just as it may be read in the Chamberlain's and Corporation
books of Stratford, for it needs no comment, no filling up
of outlines, to give it pathos and interest.

And of Shakspere himself, we know less than even this.
A few anecdotes by Aubrey and others,* all probably with

* Gossiping old Aubrey's account is as follows:—"Mr. William Shakspere was borne at Stratford-upon-Avon, in the county of Warwick. His
father was a butcher; and I have been told heretofore by some of the
neighbours, that when he was a boy he exercised his father's trade; but
when he kill'd a calfe, he would doe it in a high style, and make a speech.
There was at that time another butcher's son in this towne, that was held
not at all inferior to him for a naturall witt, his acquaintance and coetanean,
but dyed young. This Wm., being inclined naturally to poetry and acting,
came to London, I guesse about 18, and was an actor at one of the play-

some little glimmering of truth, but all going to prove his
extreme poverty when first turned adrift in the world; a
few obscure passages in contemporary writers, showing
how quickly he rose to fame, is all that we know of him.
In a manuscript list of the quantity of corn and malt in
Stratford, in February, $\frac{1597}{1598}$, a time of great dearth, we find
Shakspere possessing the large quantity of ten quarters,
and learn from the ward in which his name appears that
he was living at New Place.*   In the Chamberlain's books
for the same year we meet with the following:—

"Pd. to Mr. Shaxspere for on lod of ston.   . . x*d*."

And in a letter of the date of January, $\frac{1597}{1598}$, preserved
amongst the documents of the Stratford Town Council, we
find his name mentioned as likely to purchase land at Shottery, proving that he was now a man of wealth and means.
And this, with one or two other incidental notices in other
letters, is all we know of him.   No document belonging to
Shakspere ever turns up, with one exception, a letter to
him from Richard Quiney, which, when I last saw it, was in

---

houses, and did act exceedingly well. Now, B. Johnson was never a good
actor, but an excellent instructor. He began early to make essayes at
dramatique poetry, which at that time was very lowe, and his plays took
well.   He was a handsome, well-shap't man, very good company, and of a
very readie and pleasant smooth wit," &c.

* This list, as well as the next letter, is quoted in full by Mr. Halliwell,
pp. 167, 172.

the possession of the late Mr. Wheler, of Stratford, and which I shall venture to give in full :—

"Loveinge contreyman, I am bolde of you, as of a ffrende, cravinge your helpe with xxx. *li.* uppon Mr. Bushells and my securitee, or Mr. Myttens with me. Mr. Rosswell is nott come to London as yeate, and I have especiall cawse. You shall ffrende me muche in helpeinge me out of all the debettes I owe in London, I thanck God, and muche quiet my mynde, which wolde nott be indebted. I am nowe towardes the Cowrte, in hope of answer for the dispatche of my buyseness. You shall nether loose creddyt nor monney by me, the Lorde wyllinge ; and nowe butt perswade yourselfe soe, as I hope, and you shall nott need to feare, butt, with all hartie thanckefullnes, I wyll holde my tyme, and content your ffrende, and yf we bargaine further, you shal be the paie-master yourselfe. My tyme biddes me hastin to an ende, and soe I committ thys (to) yowr care and hope of yowr helpe. I feare I shall not be backe thys night ffrom the Cowrte. Haste. The Lorde be with yow and with us all, Amen! ffrom the Bell in Carter Lane, the 25 October, 1598.

"Yowrs in all kyndenes,

"RYCH. QUYNEY."

"To my lovinge good ffrend and contreyman Mr. Wm. Shackespere deliver theese."

This is the only scrap of paper which we know for
certain that we possess that Shakspere ever read.   It is
a precious document—one short glimpse which we catch
of the poet.   I see not the slightest ground for the conjecture, which has been founded upon it, that Shakspere at
one period of his life was a money-lender.   "Loving good
friend," and "loving countryman," is not quite, I should
suppose, the way in which a usurer would be addressed
upon money matters at any period of the world's history.
Nor does the tone of the rest of the note countenance the
supposition.   Better, surely, is it for us to regard this
letter as showing Shakspere in the light of a friend
helping a friend, possessed with that love, which is so
marked in all his writings, and that sympathy which is
the finest trait in our human nature.

Shakspere's Desk

Charlecote Hall.

CHAPTER VI.

CHARLECOTE PARK.

As I noticed in the first chapter, how happy a circumstance it was that Shakspere's birth should have fallen in the very heart of England; so, too, do I think it was no less a happy event that it should have happened in the month of April, in "the sweet of the year," and that the flowers should both be blooming when he was born and when he died. It is no mere idle fancy. If there be any truth in the

definition that poetry is " the unison of man with nature,"
then, I repeat, it *is* a happy event that the greatest poet
should have been born in nature's sweetest time.   As a
much inferior man to Shakspere, Jean Paul Richter used
to say, " I, the Professor, and the Spring came together,"
and if he should think this a happy circumstance with
regard to himself, let us, too, not doubt it with respect to
Shakspere.

Therefore, it shall be April when we will go amongst the
fields — where we know Shakspere must have rambled.
I suppose every one knows the story of the deer-poaching
at Charlecote Park ; how, so it runs, Shakspere was
caught in the very act, and brought before the old knight,
and how, in revenge, the future poet wrote, and fixed to
the park-gates, some doggerel, of which I can only say
with the German commentators, that it is more marked for
Aristophanic abuse than for wit or poetical beauty, and, in
consequence, was obliged to fly his home. *   Well, to-day,

---

* There are two versions of this doggerel; the one most commonly known
purporting to be from the MS. notes of Oldys, is as follows:—

> A parliament member, a justice of peace,
> At home a poor scarecrow, at London an asse;
> If lousie is Lucy, as some volke miscalle it,
> Then Lucy is lousie, whatever befalle it:
>> He thinkes himselfe greate,
>> Yet an asse in his state,
> We allowe by his eares but with asses to mate:

on Shakspere's birthday will we go to this old Charlecote
Park.   Our way lies over the bridge across the Avon.
The sides of the river, close up to the bridge, are fringed
with large marigolds, with their golden shadows floating
on the water, and the osier twigs in the aits are tipped
with budding silver, where the Warwickshire peasant even
now believes that the swallows hide themselves during the
winter.   The road, for the most part of the way, skirts the
river-side.   On the hedge-banks, the primroses and violets
are nestling in the warm places, and the hedge itself is just
dappled with green, whilst here and there the leafless
boughs of the blackthorn are completely crusted with
flowers.   The wryneck, the cuckoo's mate, as the Warwickshire country people call the bird, is singing close to

---

> If Lucie is lousie, as some volke miscalle it,
> Sing lousie Lucy, whatever befalle it.

Subsequently, some other modern stanzas were fabricated and joined on
to this.   The other version, said to have been gathered from an old woman,
by Professor Barnes, of Cambridge, thus runs:—

> Sir Thomas was too covetous,
>   To covet so much deer,
> When horns upon his head
>   Most plainly did appear.
> Had not his worship one deer left?
>   What then?   He had a wife
> Took pains enough to find him horns,
>   Should last him during life.

in an elm; and the cuckoo himself is calling his name afar
off.   On through the little village of Alveston we pass,
leaving Alveston pastures to the right, where, later in the
year, grow columbines, of which Ophelia speaks, blue, and
purple, and white.   And now at last, in the distance, rise up
the tall elms of Charlecote, and we presently come to a
footpath which will lead us through an angle of the park.
This is Charlecote, and the Lucys still live here.   It is like
many more fine old places dotted all over England, and
it would be, like them, equally unknown and uncared for,
but for Shakspere.   Little could the old knight have ever
dreamt that, but for that poacher, he would never have been
remembered.   He, too, would have gone the way of all the
other knights and squires of the Lucys.   But now Charlecote and the name of the Lucys will live for ever as
connected with Shakspere.   Singular, too, this poaching
business in connection with higher matters.   But perhaps
for that one circumstance we should never have had
Hamlets and Lears.   For from all we know of Shakspere, there was no particle of ambition in his mind.   He
wrote not for fame.   He cared not even to collect his
works when written.   There they were; care for them
who might.   He was indifferent to all vanity on the
subject.   He simply was content to do his duty in that
state of life in which his calling lay; and he was first

driven into it not from choice, but, as far as we can tell, from sheer necessity.

Of late years it has become the fashion to throw discredit on this poaching story. It will not do for Shakspere to be made out a common poacher. No doubt whatever, that deer-stealing was a far more venial affair than it is now. But, the story itself, if considered as the account of a wild youthful frolic, there is no reason whatever to disbelieve. That there *is* a certain basis of truth in it may be gathered from Shakspere's own writings. As a young man, he seems to have delighted in those sports, in which our forefathers, and, in fact, all Englishmen, have ever been famous. In his earliest piece, the *Venus and Adonis*, he describes a horse in all his points; whilst in the *Midsummer Night's Dream* the hounds are equally well drawn. Nor is this the slight matter that it may appear. Shakspere's writings are always fresh and healthy, and much of this is owing to the free play with which he seems to have developed the physical along with the spiritual man. Take the description of hare-hunting in the *Venus and Adonis*—

And when thou hast on foot the purblind hare,
Mark the poor wretch, to overshoot his troubles,
How he outruns the wind, and with what care
He cranks and crosses, with a thousand doubles:

The many musits * through the which he goes,
Are like a labyrinth to amaze his foes.

Sometimes he runs among a flock of sheep,
To make the cunning hounds mistake their smell;
And sometimes where earth-delving conies keep,
To stop the loud pursuers in their yell:
    And sometimes sorteth † with a herd of deer:
    Danger deviseth shifts; wit waits on fear;

For there his smell with others being mingled,
The hot-scent-snuffing hounds are driven to doubt,
Ceasing their clamorous cry till they have singled,
With much ado, the cold fault cleanly out:
    Then do they spend their mouths: Echo replies,
    As if another chase were in the skies.

By this poor Wat, far off upon a hill,
Stands on his hinder legs with listening ear,
To hearken if his foes pursue him still:
Anon their loud alarums he doth hear:
    And now his grief may be compared well
    To one woe-sick, that hears the passing bell.

Then shalt thou see the dew-bedabbled wretch
Turn, and return, indenting with the way;
Each envious brier his weary legs doth scratch:
Each shadow makes him stop, each murmur stay;
    For misery is trodden on by many,
    And being low, never relieved by any.

This description of the run is wonderfully true; how the
" dew-bedabbled wretch " betakes himself to a flock of

---

* Gaps in the hedges.   † Consorteth.

sheep to lead the hounds off the scent; how she stops to listen, and again makes another double. Mark, too, the beauty and aptness of the epithets, " the hot-scent-snuffing " hounds, and the " earth-delving " conies; but more especially mark the pity that the poet feels for the poor animal, showing that he possessed a true feeling heart, without which no line of poetry can ever be written.

But returning to the deer-poaching—the matter is, in fact, substantiated by the character of Justice Shallow, who is evidently drawn from the old Knight of Charlecote, with " a dozen white luces " in his coat of arms, which the family still bear, though not in quite such numbers. Dante we know used to put his foes into hell, and Michael Angelo to paint them there, and even Milton alludes to his enemies in the *Paradise Lost*, and surely we may excuse Shakspere for taking revenge on his old prosecutor, especially in so playful a manner. The first Act of the *Merry Wives of Windsor* is well worth reading, as we sit beneath the elms in the park. Here is a passage or two which has evidently some connection with the place :—

Master Page.   I am glad to see your worship is well; I thank
You for my venison, Master Shallow.

Justice Shallow.   Master Page, I am glad to see you; much good do it
your heart!
I wished your venison better: it was ill killed.

4

I cannot help thinking that there is a double meaning in these last words of "ill killed," a naïve allusion to former days, which at the time would be understood by more than one living person. The old Justice is drawn in a frank and kindly spirit. He loves Master Page: "I love you always with my heart: ha! with my heart." And then they fall to talking about Page's "fallow greyhound who was outrun at Cotsall," that is, on the Cotswold hills, and still so called by the Warwickshire peasant, and which may be seen from the roof of Charlecote House. And then Falstaff comes and joins them, "who has beaten the Justice's men, and killed his deer, and broken open his lodge, but not kissed the keeper's daughter;" but all is taken and given in good part. The "hot venison pasty" comes in for dinner, and Master Page hopes "we shall drink down all unkindness."

Surely in all this, and in the mention of Falstaff's "coney-catching rascalls," there is some allusion to the past; but we will trust with Master Page that the Knight and Shakspere drank down all unkindness; at least we know Shakspere was not the man to bear malice against any one.

Again, too, in the Second Part of *King Henry IV.* (act iii. scene 2), we meet with the old Justice, who mentions his friend, Will Squele, "a Cotswold man;" and the allusion to the Knight is as marked as ever by Falstaff's saying, "if the young dace be a bait for the old pike, I see no reason in the law of Nature, but I may snap at him," a luce being a full-grown pike, and snap at him Falstaff does, taking off all his peculiarities in such a way as to make him a character that will last for all time.*

And now that we are in the park, let us linger for a little. The red gables of the hall peep through the still bare elms, where the rooks are cawing above their nests; the Avon flows silently through the park, and troops of deer are winding down to its banks; the place itself in all its main features is unaltered from Shakspere's day; the great gates flanked by their stone towers, leading from the park into the courtyard, are still standing; and the house itself, the exterior at least, is much the same, with its stone-casemated windows, and its octagon towers at each corner crowned with their vanes; and inside the old hall still remains with its wide fireplace, and its deep bay

---

* This view is also supported by a statement quoted by Mr. Halliwell from the MSS. of the Rev. Richard Davies, who died in 1708, at Corpus Christi College, Oxford, " that Sir —— Lucy made Shakspere fly his native country to his great advancement; but his revenge is so great, that he is his Justice Clodpate, and calls him a great man, and that in allusion to his name bore three louses rampant for his arms."

window blazoned with armorial bearings, in which the memorable luces are conspicuous.*

And as we gaze on the scene, the imagination will go back to the old times, and we can see the hawking party setting out in the morning with its long train, and the favourite little merlin perched on its mistress's wrist, and the falconers with their gyrs and their lanners; and so they pass on under the old elms, never again to be seen.

It is useless speculating on Shakspere's offence, for we know nothing but the bare tradition, which, as we have seen, has probably some basis of truth. Whether he was captured, or what punishment he suffered, we know not; one local tradition, by the way, makes the scene of the exploit to have been Fulbrook deer-park, which, as Mr. Knight has shown, did not come into the possession of the Lucy family till after Shakspere's death. Certain it is that this incident, combined, perhaps, with his father's declining fortune, caused Shakspere to leave Stratford. What he first did in London we know not; there is the story that he held horses for people at the theatre-doors, but this, like the tale of Homer being a

* In Dugdale's *Warwickshire* (Thomas's edition, 1730), there is a view given of Charlecote, with its formal gardens, and its rows of trees, and straight walks, just as it appeared in Shakspere's day.

beggar and blind, is only a popular exaggeration of his poverty, and the hardships that every poet must go through.

Well, then, as we lie on the grass, let us take up old Drayton, who knew Warwickshire well, and thus sings of deer-hunting—not at Charlecote, but at Arden, only some twelve miles off:—

> How when the hart doth hear
> The often-bellowing hounds to scent his secret lair,
> He, rousing, rusheth out, and through the brakes doth drive,
> As though up by the roots the bushes he would rive:
> And through the cumbrous thicks as fearfully he makes,
> He with his branched head the tender sapling shakes,
> That sprinkling their moist pearls, do seem for him to weep,
> When after goes the cry with yelling loud and deep;
> That all the forest rings, and every neighbouring place,
> And there is not a hound but falleth to the chase;
> Rechating with his horn, which then the hunter cheers,
> While still the lusty stag his high-palmed head uprears.

And then, after some more lines of description—how the deer takes to the open country, and tries the brooks and the ponds—Drayton relates how the ploughman—

> His team he letteth stand,
> To assail him with his goad; so, with his hook in hand,
> The shepherd him pursues, and to his dog doth hollo,
> When, with tempestuous speed, the hounds and huntsmen follow.

The poor thing next tries the villages, but it is too late: he turns in a last effort upon his foes:—

> The churlish-throated hounds then holding him at bay,
> And, as their cruel fangs on his harsh skin they lay,
> With his sharp-pointed head he dealeth deadly wounds.
> The hunter, coming in to help his wearied hounds,
> He desperately assails: until, oppressed by force,
> He, who the mourner is to his own dying corse,
> Upon the ruthless earth his precious tears lets fall.

This is vigorous writing, but it is very poor compared with what Shakspere puts into the mouth of one of the lords in *As You Like It* (act ii. scene 1), where the scene is in the same Warwickshire Forest of Arden :—

> Under an oak, whose antique root peeps out
> Upon the brook that brawls along this wood;
> To the which place a poor sequestered stag
> That from the hunter's aim had ta'en a hurt,
> Did come to languish; and, indeed, my lord,
> The wretched animal heaved forth such groans
> That their discharge did stretch his leathern coat
> Almost to bursting; and the big round tears
> Cours'd one another down his innocent nose
> In piteous chase; and thus, the hairy fool,
> Much marked of by the melancholy Jaques,
> Stood on the extremest verge of the swift brook,
> Augmenting it with tears.

Mark here how the speaker turns away from the chase itself and the excitement of the sport, to the poor animal, wounded and dying, and weeping almost human tears; and notice too how Jaques invests the whole with a human sympathy, explaining and interpreting by it human affairs :—

First, for his weeping in the needless stream,
Poor deer, quoth he, *thou mak'st a testament*
As worldlings do, giving thy sum of more
To that which had too much. Then being alone,
Left and abandoned of his velvet friends:
'Tis right, quoth he; *thus misery doth part*
The flux of company. Anon, a careless herd,
Full of the pasture, jumps along by him,
And never stays to greet him. *Ay,* quoth Jaques,
Sweep on, you fat and greasy citizens,
'Tis just the fashion. Wherefore do you look
Upon that poor and broken bankrupt there?

This is true poetry, looking upon all things with love and pity, that can see nothing suffering pain without profound sorrow, and which, too, exalts Nature by making her the interpreter of human life and human griefs.

But we must leave the old park, and go out again into the road; and, passing the new church of Charlecote, where still remains the white marble effigy of the old Justice in full armour, and then on through Hampton Lucy, we reach the right bank of the river, and wander on towards Hatton Rock. Very beautiful indeed is Hatton Rock, with its wood sloping down to the Avon. It is full of all the spring flowers—orchisses, and oxlips, and primroses, as if April had stolen some from her sister May. There are white and pink wind-flowers still blossoming, and the bluest and sweetest violets, whilst the leaves of the bluebell cover the ground with their grass. And all the birds of spring have come here, and loud above them all, even in the middle of the day, the nightingale is singing; but the oaks and the ash show not a single bud, as if not quite certain that the warm weather had really set in.

But we must continue our walk under Rheon Hill, and so on, still by the bank of the river. The wheat in the corn-fields is now about as high as grass at midsummer, but of a darker, richer green than ever grass is; whilst the meadows are golden with buttercups. And so, at last, we reach the Warwick road, and find ourselves at Stratford, and see the flags flying, and hear the bells ringing, in honour of the day.

It is something to ponder on, that men should keep this day, and that they should come year after year to the annual dinner at Stratford. It may not be a very æsthetic mode of celebrating a poet's birthday; yet men are but men, and ordinary mortals but ordinary mortals. It is something as it is; we will not ask for more: it is hero-worship in the best way that men at present know. But it is something more to rejoice at, that on this night a festival in honour of the poet is held some three thousand miles away at New York; and the thought arises, as our Saxon language spreads, where will Shakspere's influence stop? Already is our tongue lisped in backwoods and desert places ; and there, surely, too, will Shakspere some day help to conquer the material world : with the Bible and with Shakspere we can never go back.

Autograph and Seal of Sir Thomas Lucy.

Stratford, from Welcombe Grounds

CHAPTER VII.

WELCOMBE AND SNITTERFIELD.

WHILST it is still spring — still " proud-pied April," as Shakspere beautifully calls his natal month—we will wander to some more of the places connected with his name. You can go nowhere round Stratford that is not associated with him. It is to me always a most enjoyable feeling, to know

I am breathing the air that Shakspere breathed, and am wandering where he wandered, and where he must have felt " all the mighty ravishment of Spring." To-day we will go to Welcombe. Our road lies by the back of the town, and then through fields, until we reach what are called the " dingles "—trenches, most probably, formed, in the first place, by natural causes, and then artificially deepened. Shakspere must have often come this way, for his father possessed property a little farther on, at Snitterfield. And here, still in the Welcombe grounds, stand old gnarled thorn-trees, to-day just budding, which the poet must have seen. They are, above all, worth preserving, for they are probably the only trees in the neighbourhood old enough to have existed in his time, now that the " one elm " boundary-tree on the Birmingham road has been destroyed.

The Dingles and Welcombe are closely connected with Shakspere. For it happened that in 1614 an attempt was made to enclose them, with other lands at Bishopton and Clopton, which Shakspere, who had bought the lease of the tithes, and the corporation of Stratford, successfully resisted. And in a memorandum, dated " 1614, Jovis, 17 No.," formerly in the possession of the late Mr. Wheler, we find that Shakspere told his cousin Greene, the clerk of the corporation, who had been sent to London on the matter, that the "dyngles" were not to be enclosed;* whilst in another document, quoted by Mr. Bell, with the date of the 1st September, 1615, he is represented as saying that " he was not able to bear the enclosing of Welcombe."

To-day everything is full of beauty. The lambs are leaping from land to land. The larch's purple tufts are just hardening into fir-cones; and the large pale stars of the primroses are shining brilliantly on the hedge banks; and down in the hedge ditch the arum is lifting its one spike, the " long purple " of Ophelia,—

> That liberal shepherds give a grosser name;
> But our cold maids do dead men's fingers call them;

and by these names is it known to this day to the Warwickshire peasant boy and girl.†   But the passage is of

---

* I trust that the valuable collection of documents referring to Shakspere made by the late Mr. Wheler, will be carefully preserved, and never allowed to leave Stratford.   They are by far the most interesting of any that I know in private hands.   The memorandum referred to runs as follows:—" 1614 Jovis, 17 No.   My cosen Shakspear comyng yesterdy to town, I went to see him how he did.   He told me that they assured him they ment to inclose no further than to Gospell Bush, and so upp straight (leavying out part of the dyngles to the ffield) to the gate in Clopton hedg, and take in Salisburyes peece; and that they mean in Aprill to survey the land, and then to gyve satisfaccion, and not before: and he and Mr. Hall say they think ther will be nothyng done at all."

† I know that there are several interpretations of " long-purples."   Miss Baker, in her excellent *Glossary of Northamptonshire Words*, conceives it

more value than as a reference to local names, for it shows the instinctive delicacy of Shakspere's mind.   He will not put even into the wicked queen's mouth the gross country name.   He is as delicate as the most refined lady.

Come on a little farther, to the brow of the hill, where, when Shakspere was dead, was fought one of the skirmishes in the Civil War, and where men have been dug up, buried, in hot haste, in their armour, with their swords by their sides, just as they fell.   Come, we have soon reached the top of the hill, and are now in a grass-field, where we shall see Ophelia's "crow-flowers," by which name the butter-cup (*ranunculus bulbosus*) is still called in Warwickshire, and must not be confounded with the

---

to be the purple loosestrife of the river side.   I have no doubt whatever that this latter bears this name, as well as the arum, but it does not, happily, also bear the grosser name.   Besides, Shakspere, with his wonderful accuracy in describing Nature, would not have mixed the loosestrife, a summer plant, with "the crow-flowers, nettles, and daisies," all of them spring flowers, which also is the arum.   Some commentators say that the orchis is the flower intended; but it is not nearly so like a dead man's fingers as the livid, purple, flabby, finger-like flower of the arum.   Besides, about Stratford, at least, the orchis is always called "king's-fingers."   But the names of "dead man's fingers and thumb" are common in various parts of the country to other plants.   Thus, the fumitory is called "bloody man's thumb" in some places, and the musk-hyacinth "dead man's thumb," as in the old song:—

> Such flowers which in the meadow grew,
> The dead man's thumb and harebell blue.

crow-foot (*ranunculus arvensis*), of which Mr. Tennyson
writes—

> The cowslip and the crow-foot are over all the hill;

and which Milton calls "the tufted crow-toe," the "dill-
cup" or "yellow-cress" of the more southern counties, but
which does not bloom till the middle of May. We shall
find, too, all the flowers mentioned in *Love's Labour Lost*
(act v. scene 2):—

> The daisies pied, and violets blue,
>   And ladies'-smocks all silver white,
> And cuckoo-buds of yellow hue,
>   Which paint the meadows with delight.

The cuckoo-buds are still in Warwickshire now, as in
Shakspere's time—the lesser celandines, which are in full
bloom when the cuckoo comes. And the ladies'-smocks,
also, are called cuckoo-flowers, for the cuckoo is a favourite
bird with the English peasant. And a little later in the
spring we should see pansies peeping through the grass,
still called throughout the midland counties, as in the
Midsummer Night's Dream (act ii. scene 2), love-in-
idleness, but in the more southern counties simply, love-
and-idle.

To me there is always something very beautiful in the
names with which the peasants christen their flowers and
their birds. There is ever something so simple, yet

characteristic, in them, that many of them are poetry itself. And in our great poets, we always find their names faithfully preserved, as we have just seen in Shakspere's case. Take that most beautiful of all flowers, the wild columbine, which formerly grew in such abundance in our English woods and pastures, and examine its old name which has passed away, of culver-keys, used by Isaac Walton, a true prose-poet. It is exactly the same in meaning as the scientific term of *aquilegia*, only far more beautiful and expressive, " culver " signifying a dove, and having reference to the dove-like flowers taking their flight, as it were, away from their nest. And so, through the whole nomenclature of English wild flowers, our wake-robins, ladies'-tresses, daisies, and cuckoo-flowers, and gossamer (still called " gauze o' the summer" in the northern counties), were all names given by true poets, who felt the meaning and the worth of their beauty. And I dwell especially upon this, because in this generation we seem to have thrown aside all love for nature, and prefer to live, penned up like cattle, in a town, to dwelling in the country. I know not how the vast difference can be expressed in words between the times when May-day was a festival for high and low, and when a May-pole was set up in the Strand, and our present day, when London is one vast desert of pavement, with red and blackened ramparts

of hideous streets, and its outskirts one wilderness of brick-
fields; but it is a difference that is sensibly making itselt
felt in our literature.

Our road still lies through fields, and, leaving Ingon to
the right, where Shakspere's father, as we have seen, in
1570 held a small farm of about fourteen acres, called
Ingon Meadow, we reach Snitterfield, where the poet's
grandfather and uncle lived, and in the parish register
may be found entries of various members of their family;
and where the Ardens, Shakspere's mother's family, also
held property, which through his wife came to Shakspere's
father. Beyond Snitterfield are the " Bushes," now young
timber, but where probably there have been woods from
time immemorial. The wild daffodil is still shining
through the bare trees, and violets, and primroses, and
oxlips are growing so thick together that you cannot help
treading down thousands as you walk. The place where
Shakspere's father lived is now no longer known, although
tradition still points to where his house stood. But I cannot help thinking that Shakspere must have known some of
the haunts round Snitterfield. Here, more beautiful than
anywhere else, do all the flowers which bloom in his pages
still blossom. I have seen these woods, early in the cold
days of February, just in the spaces where the trees had
been cleared, covered with celandines, making a golden

sunshine on the ground when none was to be seen in the heaven; and then, when these were all gone, the earth was snowed over with white wind-flowers; and as these went, new beauty came, for now the ground was paved with clumps and tufts of primroses and patches of wood-violets; and when these, too, were gone, the hyacinths arose, encircling the trunks of the trees in a blue haze; and so one growth of beauty was ever succeeded by another, still more beauteous. I can never go into these woods in the spring time without thinking of that wondrous description in the *Winter's Tale* (act iv. scene 3):—

> O Proserpina,
> For the flowers now, that, frighted, thou let'st fall
> From Dis's waggon!—daffodils,
> That come before the swallow dares, and take
> The winds of March with beauty; violets, dim,
> But sweeter than the lids of Juno's eyes,
> Or Cytherea's breath; pale primroses,
> That die unmarried, ere they can behold
> Bright Phœbus in his strength—a malady
> Most incident to maids.

Mark the whole passage. How wonderfully accurate it is! Every flower is mentioned in the order it grows. No idle word-painting, either, is there: no superfluous, common-place epithets; no colour is laid on for mere colouring's sake, but everything goes to the very essence of the matter. You can see at once that the writer is describing, not for

mere description's sake, but from his pure, deep love of
beauty. The daffodils are simply the early flowers, that
come before the swallow, marking the advent of both, their
earliness being their chief characteristic—blooming when
nothing else blooms. And the violets, they are dim, that
is, dimly seen among their green leaves; and their essence
is not their colour—not blue or purple, as inferior poets
would have called them—but their sweetness: "sweeter
than e'en Cytherea's breath." Milton, in a well-known
passage, calls the violet "glowing;" but there is no dis-
crepancy between the two poets: one is describing the
budding violet, scarcely seen amidst its green foliage, and
the other the full-blown flower, quite purple and bright in
the sunshine. And of the primroses, he notes of them, as
Milton does, that they die so soon; not that they actually
do, for they last as long as any flower, but because we are
so sorry to lose them, that the time they have been with us
seems so very short. He calls them pale, as he does also in
Cymbeline, probably for two reasons: first, because they
are pale, when compared with the deep gold of the celan-
dine, close to which they so often grow; and secondly,
because round Stratford a red variety is found, and
the country-people, to distinguish them, as in other
parts of England, call them respectively red and white
primroses.

Through these "Bushes," too, runs the old lane, where Charles II. rode, disguised as Jane Lane's servant, in flight after the battle of Worcester, and to this day one portion of the lane is called King's Lane, and not many years ago the peasant would have pointed you out an oak under which the fugitive is said to have taken shelter. But the old lane is now nearly destroyed, and we shall do better to try the fields. So, leaving the farm-house of Cummings behind us, with its gorse cover, now golden with blossoms, we find ourselves once more on the same ridge of hills of which Welcombe is a continuation. Let us sit here on the stile for a little while. It is the most beautiful, but least known, of all the views round Stratford. I could sit here for hours. Below us lies the real country of Shakspere, outrolled like a map. Take away the canal and the two railroads, and it is essentially the same that Shakspere saw. The hills are the same. And Avon rolls on the same through the midst. And the same gray clouds come moving day after day across the heavens; and the sun sets down the same.

Let us look at it once more, for it is as beautiful a picture of quiet English scenery as can be found anywhere, and when joined with the name of Shakspere, becomes doubly beautiful. No one, I suppose, could look upon Thermopylæ without feeling some glow of patriotism, and no one, surely, can look upon this scene without experiencing some feelings of poetry. Before us rise the Cotswold Hills, with their outlyer, Meon, with its " copped " head, to use a word of Shakspere's, its sides still covered with wood; and, more to the right, Binton, with its mounded terraces, under which the Avon flows, fettering hamlet to hamlet with its silver links; and, farther off, the long back of Bredon ; and, still farther, the two peaks of Malvern, cleaving the clear air. And nearer to us lies Wimpcote, where Shakspere's mother lived, and where his father held the farm of Ashbies; and Shottery, nestling amongst elms ; whilst Stratford and its church are steeped in the golden sunlight.

Well, we must now return to the old town. The pathway goes down the hill, and then by the side of high hedges, where the wild pear and apple-trees are now blossoming; one of the most striking features in springtime of Warwickshire and the Midland districts. On through Lower Clopton, and then crossing the lane, past Clopton House, of which John Combe's daughter was once the mistress. The house has been entirely rebuilt, excepting a portion of the back, where the curious old entrance-gate still stands, and under which Shakspere and John Combe may often have passed. On down Clopton Lane, and so into the main road, where stood the "one elm," a parish boundary mark, which we know by parish documents was standing in Shakspere's time. But it has been destroyed. We really seem in these days to have lost all reverence for the past. Herne's oak at Windsor was cut down, either through negligence or wilfulness. And now this old elm is gone. It might have been spared as long as it would stand, to have yearly put forth its few green leaves, and that the passer-by might have said, " Shakspere saw this tree."

Welcombe Thorns.

Anne Hathaway's Cottage

CHAPTER VIII.

SHOTTERY.

IF there be one place more interesting than another in
connection with Shakspere, it is the little hamlet of
Shottery, for here he found his wife. It lies but a few
fields' length from Stratford—one of the prettiest of English villages. Very lovely is it always in April—in "the
winter of the blackthorn," as the Warwickshire country-

people call the season. It consists of but a few cottages and farm-houses, straggling here and there, with their gardens full of flowers. The white snowdrops, and the crocuses that had fringed the beds with a border of flame, are all gone, though a few daffodils still remain; but the oxlips, and the primroses, and the jonquil on its slender rush, are shining bright, whilst the turk's-cap lilies, and the tulips, and the columbines, are all springing up, covering the earth with their green leaves, and the apple-trees are just opening their pink rose-buds, and the pears and the cherry-trees are covered with their white May blossoms.

At the far end of the village, down in a little valley, where runs the village brooklet, stands Anne Hathaway's cottage. An old, long, timbered house is it, its front chequered with squares, where the vine now stretches its cane-coloured naked arms, its stones crusted with moss, and its thatch, too, green with tufts and clumps of moss. Inside it is nothing more than a simple English cottage, with its high mantel-shelf ornamented with a bright row of candlesticks and earthenware, and its clean floor of Binton stone, sunk and cracked in places. And its garden is simply an English cottage garden, such as you may see thousands of in Warwickshire, but still none the less beautiful, with its well and its wallflowers, and its lavender-shrubs, and kitchen herbs. And behind stands a small orchard, which, if it be an early season, will be a mass of pink blossom, whilst the meadows beyond are covered with cowslips.

All this was here in Shakspere's time. There was the same beauty in the old world as is now. Nothing can alter that. And, doubtless, to Shakspere this place and these fields were, above all others, the most beautiful, for he had seen them through the inspiration of love.

Upon Shakspere's house doubts have been thrown, but upon this no shade of suspicion rests. The traveller can believe with a full faith that here Shakspere, when a young man, came and won his wife. It is something to think of, that Shakspere's helpmate—the woman who above every one else influences a man's life for either extreme good or utter evil—here dwelt. I cannot enter into that barren controversy as to who she was, or what her father might be, but of this do I feel certain, that she influenced Shakspere's mind for good, and not for harm. There is, I know, that base theory, for I can call it nothing else, that Shakspere and his wife lived on bad terms. Verily the world is hard upon its greatest men. And what is the foundation for this belief? Simply because in his will Shakspere left her only his second best bed. Perhaps from husband to wife there was no more precious bequest: the bed whereon they had slept for years, where their children had been born to them, and where they themselves might hope to die in peace and quietness. I would myself sooner believe in the creeds of South Sea Islanders than in such utter baseness of thought. If there is one thing Shakspere dwells upon more than another it is the duty and love of husband and wife, and of children to parents. To suppose that he was at variance with his wife, is to suppose that he must have ever been giving the lie to his own thoughts. The man who asked—

> What nearer debt in all humanity
> Than wife to husband?

was the man who could best answer the question. There really does seem a sort of epidemic of base belief, among men, which loves to traduce the world's heroes. If one thing be certain, it is that Shakspere was a good man— including under it a good husband. It is no paradox to say that a good poet must be a good man. The reason (*Vernunft*) can only flourish with moral truth. It is as true now as it was two thousand years ago, that ἡ ἀρετὴ ποιητοῦ συνέζευκται τῇ τοῦ ἀνθρώπου, καὶ οὐκ οἶον τε ἀγαθόν γενέσθαι ποιητὴν μὴ πρότερον γενηθέντα ἄνδρα ἀγαθόν. Not until the experiment of brambles bringing forth figs succeeds, will the still greater miracle of a bad man writing true poetry come to pass. For poetry is, after all, nothing but the reflex of the spiritual nature of a man. And I feel sure of this, that Shakspere's vast superiority over his fellow-dramatists sprang not so much from his intellect as from his higher moral power.

Even Ulrici and the best German critics fall into this common error of Shakspere living on bad terms with his wife, perhaps not knowing, as Mr. Knight first showed, that she was already provided for by her dowry, and there was therefore no occasion for her to be mentioned in his will. There is, however, direct testimony of at least her love for her husband, which has been previously quoted, in her affecting and touching wish to be buried with him in his grave.

To suppose that Shakspere and his wife had no griefs, no embitterments, is to suppose what never happened to two people on this earth. But griefs, if wisely taken, only the more endear affection; and that was, no doubt, the use to which Shakspere turned his trials and afflictions. Life, whether wedded or unwedded, is action springing from suffering; and the greater the man, and the finer and tenderer his conscience, the more he realizes this truth.

Avon at the Weir Brake.

CHAPTER IX.

THE AVON—LUDDINGTON—WELFORD.

WE must wait till midsummer to go by the side of the
Avon, for then it is in its greatest beauty. So, on some
warm day in June will we go. There is a path on both
sides of the river, but we will pass over the foot-bridge
at the mill, and ascend "the cross of the Hill," for here
we shall find a spot curiously connected with Shakspere.

"I beseech you, sir," says Davy to Justice Shallow, in the second part of *King Henry IV.* (act v. scene 1), "to countenance William Visor of Wincot against Clement Perkes of the Hill;" to whom the Justice replies: "There are many complaints, Davy, against that Visor; that Visor is an arrant knave on my knowledge." Now the Cherry-Orchard Farm, close to which we are, is still called the Hill Farm; and whoever lives there is to this day spoken of as Mr. A., or Mr. B., of the Hill, and is so named from time immemorial in the Weston parish register. Whilst Wincot is still the name of a farm some three miles to the left, where, probably, there was once a village, the same Wincot where Christopher Sly runs fourteenpence in debt with Marian Hacket for "sheer ale," or rather "Warwickshire ale," as Mr. Collier's corrector proposes, and of which reading I suppose all Warwickshire people will approve.* Depend upon it all these

---

* In Cokain's *Small Poems*, published in 1658, may be found a curious epigram, addressed to Mr. Clement Fisher, of Wincot, referring to Christopher Sly:—

> Shakspere your Wincot ale hath much renown'd,
> That fox'd a beggar so (by chance was found
> Sleeping), that there needed not many a word
> To make him believe he was a lord:
> But you affirm, and in it seem most eager,
> 'Twill make a lord as drunk as any beggar.

people really existed—good Justice Shallow, and Davy his servant, and Marian Hacket and her daughter Cicely, at Wincot ale-house, and Clement Perkes of the Hill, and many a laugh would they and Shakspere have at these scenes.

I know how dangerous it is to theorise on such points as these, and that Shakspere never drew mere individuals but always types of men. Still I cannot help thinking that good, gossiping Aubrey might have hit upon the truth when he tells us that Shakspere drew his characters from the different persons that he met; and adds that the Constable in the *Midsummer Night's Dream* (he probably meant either Dogberry or Verges in *Much Ado about Nothing*) was drawn from a certain constable at Grendon, in Buckinghamshire, where Shakspere stayed one Midsummer night on his road from London to Stratford. We have already seen that he drew his Justice Shallow

---

Did Norton brew such ale as Shakspere fancies
Did put Kit Sly into such lordly trances?
And let us meet there for a fit of gladness,
And drink ourselves merry in sober sadness.

Norton is said to have been the landlord of the Falcon Inn, at Bidford, famous for being the scene of Shakspere's well-known drinking bout, where Sir Aston Cokain and his friends used also to meet. It may have been from some confusion about this sonnet and the Falcon Inn, that the popular tradition, mentioned a little further on in the text about the Induction to the *Taming of the Shrew*, had its origin.

from the old knight at Charlecote, and in the Oldys MSS.
it is said that the character of Falstaff was drawn from
a fellow-townsman of Shakspere's; and popular tradition
in Warwickshire asserts that the Induction to the *Taming
of the Shrew* had its origin in a joke played off by some
member of Sir Aston Cokain's family upon a tinker in
Shakspere's time.   This may have been the case, but
the joke is an old one, and to be found in literature long
before.   But it is worth while noting, with Mr. Halliwell,
that many of the names in Shakspere's plays, such as
Bardolf, Fluellin, Sly, Herne (or as it stood in the first
draft of the *Merry Wives of Windsor*, Horne), Page,
Ford, &c., may all be found in the corporation books of
Stratford, and were the names of people living there in
Shakspere's day.

Perhaps, though, this mention of the " Hill Farm " and
Wincot so close together, and the satire upon Justice
Shallow, is the most marked instance of Shakspere alluding
to matters which may be supposed to be generally known
at the time.   But in his plays there are other places in
the neighbourhood of Stratford mentioned.   I have alluded
to Master Slender's speaking of " Cotsall," the pronunciation still in vogue by the peasantry for the Cotswold hills.
So, too, when mentioning Kenilworth, in the Second Part
of *King Henry VI.* (act iv. scene 4), we find Shakspere

calling it by the old term of Killingworth, a pronunciation which the common people still adopt. So, too, in the Induction to the *Taming of the Shrew*, the village of Burton Heath, where Christopher Sly was born, should probably be written Barton-on-the-Heath, a small village some ten or twelve miles from Stratford, and most probably the place meant by Silence in the Second Part of *King Henry IV.* (act v. scene 3), where he speaks of " goodman Puff of Barson," the popular corruption of Barton, in the neighbourhood. That Shakspere should have alluded to his native county, and to the places amongst which he spent his earliest days, was but natural. That in his exile in London he still loved them, we know from Aubrey's evidence, for he used to go " to his native countrey once a yeare; " and from the fact that when he had made his fortune he retired to his birthplace to spend his last days.

But, on the other hand, we may be sure that wherever Shakspere travelled, or wherever he was, he worked up all he saw into his poems. No colour in the sky, but he painted it on his canvas; no tree or flower, but he grafted its beauty on his verse. No old snatch, or saw, or " trivial fond record," which he heard, but, like his own Hamlet, he copied it within " the book and volume of his brain." The old tradition, that he was a miser, and saved up every penny, would be far more applicable to the riches of his mind. He saved and hoarded up all he saw or heard, and he acted just as he makes Pandarus say, in *Troilus and Cressida* (act iv. scene 4)—"Let us cast away nothing, for we may live to have need of such a verse."

We must now, though, after this long digression, come back to the river across the fields, and we shall find ourselves at the Weir Brake, a wood which covers the high banks of the Avon at its first reach from the foot-bridge. There is a tradition that this was the scene of the *Midsummer Night's Dream*. I am willing to believe it, for I do not like rooting up such old beliefs. The place is quite beautiful enough for such a scene ; only do not ask me to believe too literally, for the poet's mind wanders over all space, unconsciously gathering up all things it has ever seen or heard, and fusing them into a whole. The trees reach down from the high banks to the edge of the water, and the green fern-plumes wave themselves whenever a little breeze steals through the branches ; and the people about here still believe, as in Shakspere's time, that the fern-seed, gathered with certain rites on Midsummer-day, can make them invisible.

Very beautiful, indeed, is it about Midsummer, as we stand on the top of the bank, looking towards Stratford Church in the distance, and the river winding beneath our feet, just seen through the wood, where the vetchling

climbs up the green may-bushes, pulling her purple
blossoms along with her ; and the wind blows the sweet
scent from the bean-fields, and the laughter of the hay-
makers tedding out the hay. Surely it is a place beautiful
enough to have inspired the *Midsummer Night's Dream*,
and we will not too closely question the tradition.

There is, too, another tradition which I give only upon its
own value, that at the old moated manor-house at Radbrook, about three miles off, there used to be a large
library,—and many people still living can remember the
books there fifty years ago,—where Shakspere used to retire
to study. The old hall has long since been converted into
a farm-house, and I have never been able to learn the fate
of the library.

But we must leave the Weir Brake ; our path, though,
still lies by the side of the river lined with willows. Past
the railroad, and Stoneyford, and the river Stour, we go ;
very lovely about a month later, or even now if it is an
early season, is each reach of the river fringed with thick
purple spikes of the loosestrife, and the blue flowers of the
meadow geranium, and here and there in the swampy
places the yellow flag-flowers are shining, and the river itself
is almost dammed up with great green islands of reeds and
rushes, through which the water flows so slowly, and from
which the reed-sparrow is ever singing, and close to them

are floating the water lilies with their broad green leaves,
and their golden stars.

And now at last we are opposite Luddington, where it
is said Shakspere was married. The church has long since
been destroyed, and not only the church, but its register,
and that only a few years since, and so all traces of the
event are lost. We next pass the little church of Weston
Sands, and so reach Welford; where there still stands a
high Maypole in the village painted with red and white,
and from seeing which we may better understand poor
Helena's speech to Hermia, in the *Midsummer Night's
Dream* (act iii. scene 2):

> How low am I, thou painted Maypole? speak;
> How low am I?

Perhaps we can never rightly understand Shakspere,
unless we can throw ourselves back into the England of
Shakspere's time, when May-day, and Whitsuntide, and
sheep-shearing were real festivals, to all of which there are
such constant allusions in his plays. And even the
Midsummer Night's Dream we can but faintly comprehend
in comparison with those who first saw it performed, and
who really believed that there was a visible world of fairies,
and elves, and pyxies around them, and that on that very
night they possessed unusual spells over men.

Here at Welford luckily the parish register is still in existence, and from it I shall venture to give an extract of a flood which happened in Shakspere's lifetime, as I believe it has never been published before except in a work which is now very scarce : *—

"On the 18th day of July, 1588, in morning, there happened about eight of the clock, in Avon, such a sudden floode, as carried away all the hay about Avon. Old Father Porter, buried about four years past, being then a hundred and nine years of age, never knew it so high by a yard and a half. Dwelling in the mill-house, he, in former times, knew it under his bed, but this flood was a yard and a half in the house, and came in so suddenly that John Perry's wife was so amazed that she sate still till she was almost drowned, and was well nigh beside herself, and so far amiss that she did not know her own child when it was brought into her. It braike down Grange Mill; the crack thereof was heard at Holditch. It braike up sundry houses in Warwick town, and carried away their bread, beef, cheese, butter, pots, pans and provisions, and took away ten carts out of one town, and three wains, with the furniture of Mr. Thomas Lucies, and broke both ends of

---

* *The Shaksperian Repository*, a work which, I believe, only reached two numbers.

Stratford Bridge. That (flood) drowned three furlongs of corn in Thetford field. It was so high at the height that it unthatched the mill, and stocked up a number of willows and salles, and did take away one (of) Sales's daughters of Grafton, out of Hilborrow meadow, removing of the hay-cock, that she had no shift but to get upon the top of a hay-cock, and was carried thereupon by the water a quarter of a mile well nigh, till she came to the very last bank of the stream, and there was taken into a boat, and all was liked to be drowned, but that another boat coming rescued them soon. Three men going over Stratford-bridge, when they came to the middle of the bridge they could not go forward, and then returning presently, could not get back, for the water was so risen, it rose a yard every hour from eight to foure, that it came into the parsonage of Welford Orchard, and filled his fish-poole, and took away the sign-post at the Bare; it carried away Edward Butler's carte, and which was soon beneath Bidford, and it came into the vicarage of Weston, and made Adam Sandars thence remove, and took away half a hundred pounds of hay."

I would beg the reader to remark at the commencement of the extract the beautiful expression of Avon, without the personal article, as if the river were a friend, and not an inanimate object, a mode of speaking still in use among

the peasantry. The account of the poor miller's wife not
knowing her own child, when it was brought, is very
touching; and the whole shows that life in the sixteenth
century was much the same in respect to its joys and
sorrows as life is now. I hardly like to hazard a conjecture on a subject about which the best commentators
cannot agree; but perhaps the date of this flood may help
to fix the date of the *Midsummer Night's Dream*, and that
when Shakspere wrote,—

> The winds, piping to us in vain,
> As in revenge, have suck'd up from the sea
> Contagious fogs; which falling in the land,
> Have every pelting river made so proud,
> That they have overborne their continents :
> The ox has therefore stretch'd his yoke in vain,
> The ploughman lost his sweat; and the green corn
> Hath rotted, ere his youth attained a beard :
> The fold stands empty in the drowned field :
> The crows are fatted with the murrain flock.

He may have had this flood and its disastrous conse-
quences in his mind. The *Midsummer Night's Dream*,
though not amongst the earliest series of Shakspere's plays,
is, from the internal evidence of style, an early work, and
the first draft of it may have been produced soon after
1588, when Shakspere would be in his twenty-fifth year.

Bidford Bridge.

CHAPTER X.

"PIPING PEBWORTH—DANCING MARSTON."

I SUPPOSE there is no one who does not know the story
that Shakspere having gone over to Bidford, on a drinking
bout, was overcome with the Bidford ale, and spent the
night on his road home under a crab-tree, and in the

morning, being asked to renew the contest, refused, saying
that he had drunk with—

> Piping Pebworth, Dancing Marston,
> Haunted Hillborough, and hungry Grafton;
> With dodging Exhall, Papist Wixford,
> Beggarly Broom, and drunken Bidford.

I suppose the story, with different variations, will be
told wherever Shakspere's name is mentioned. We hear
so little about him authentic, that we make up for it by
believing in the silliest tradition. It may, or may not,
have been true. Drinking bouts or contests were very
frequent in those days, and there is no reason for sup-
posing that Shakspere, when a young man, should have
been proof against their temptations. I dare even say
that Shakspere, as Anthony Wood quaintly says of
Skelton, " was guilty of certain crimes as most poets
are." But to suppose that Shakspere was a drunkard is
an absurdity self-refuted. It is like that other foolish
tradition handed down on the authority of the good gossiping old vicar of Stratford, the Rev. John Ward, that
Shakspere died from a fever contracted by drinking. The
shallower the theory the deeper it impresses itself on
men's minds. No doubt, Shakspere, as we all do, fell into
temptation. Life is, after all, a lesson, taught us by our
mistakes ; but it is from rising after every fall, and not
grovelling on the ground, that we learn wisdom.

Since these doggerel lines are so interwoven with Shakspere's name, we may as well go to the places mentioned. And we will go in the autumn, that we may then have seen the country in each season of the year. The places all lie so scattered, that we cannot take them in the order given in the lines.

We will begin with Dancing Marston, or Marston sicca, a long straggling village, about two miles from Welford, where we stopped at in the last chapter. The lines have at least the charm of truth about them, for, to this day, Marston is celebrated for dancing, and I believe that even now, a band of morris-dancers, with their proper costumes, could be collected in the place. But Marston is known for other things beside dancing. Here Charles the Second, after the battle of Worcester, took refuge, at the Manor House of the Tomes', in whose family it still remains, and where the well-known incident of his turning the jack took place. The jack may to this day be seen, and the village tradition will tell you, how "the king fled into the kitchen, hard pursued by the Parliamentary soldiers, and the loyal kitchen-maid, to save his life, set him to turn the jack. The soldiers broke in after him. The King in his fright looked round; but the loyal maiden, still faithful, hit him on the back with the basting-ladle, adding, ' Now, go on ; and mind your work.' " The blind, so the story runs, was effectual, and the soldiers departed.*

There is a footpath across the fields to Pebworth. The corn about here is still uncut, although both stalk and ears are of a deep orange, and wave across the country like a molten sea of gold. Very sweet now is the walk through the fields by the hedgeside, where the briony, with its deep bright green leaves, is climbing the hedge, covered with its clusters of berries, and where the long bramble shoots and sprays stretch over the path, still blossomed with gray and pink flowers, and the ditch is matted with heriff and tangle-grass and ladies' bedstraw, and the first dewberry, with which Titania feeds Bottom, shows its dark purple berry silvered over with a delicate frost-like bloom.

A few fields bring us to " Piping Pebworth," which still keeps up its reputation for music. There is nothing to detain us here. And, so rambling over more fields, we reach the old Roman Icknield Street, which will lead us across the Avon into Bidford, still, I believe, as famous as ever for its love for good ale. Here at the Falcon, now turned into a poorhouse, is a room still shown as the scene of the famous festivity. Following the Stratford road for about a mile, we shall reach on the right-hand side, the

---

* For the more authentic account, see *The Boscobel Tracts*, edited by J. Hughes. London, 1857.

place where the crab-tree stood. It perished from natural decay in 1824, and nothing marks its site but an old gate-post. However, the view from here will well repay us. Before us spreads the vale of Evesham, the most fertile, perhaps, in England. The country here, which is always earlier than any other, is now in the middle of harvest. A fresh breeze, though, is blowing, here and there in play knocking down a sheaf, as if it were a huge nine-pin, and rustling the crab-apples down from the hedge-row trees, and blowing about the young second broods of birds that are taking their first lessons in flying; but, best of all, breathing cool upon the brows of the toiling harvestmen, and the poor harvestwomen, their backs aching with picking up the bundles after the reapers, whilst the Avon flows so silently down the valley.

The other places mentioned in the rhyme are all mere villages. Broom is called " beggarly," both from the poverty of its soil and its inhabitants; and " Papist " Wixford, still, I believe, belongs to the old Roman Catholic family of the Throckmortons. " Haunted ', Hillborough is now a mere farmhouse by the river-side, quite lonely enough to have the credit for being haunted. It was formerly an old manor-house, and is but little changed from what it was in Shakspere's time, with its old barns, and its old round-stone dove-house. " Dodging "

Exhall, as I venture to write, instead of the usual " dadging " Exhall, is, I must suppose, so called on account of the trouble there is to find it. I know that the first time that I went there, I was several hours before I could reach the place, and then, to use an Hibernicism, never found it; unless two or three straggling cottages make the village. The prettiest place of them all is " Hungry" Grafton, or Temple-Grafton, as it is also called, where some of the old Knights Templar once lived. But where their dwelling was, there is nothing now but a farmhouse standing very prettily amongst its elms, and you may trace by the mounds and hollows in the adjoining meadow, where had once been the fishpools of the old Knights. The epithet " hungry " is still true of the soil, which is very poor; and a farm in the parish, to this day, bears the name of Hungry Arbour Farm. There is little to be seen in the village but a few houses built of the blue lias stone of the district. We will go on. A quiet village footpath through the meadows, by the side of a brook, which flows down to the Avon, will bring us out into the Stratford road.*

But it is not these places alone that should interest us. It is the whole country. And as we go on to Stratford,

---

* For those who take a greater interest in the tradition of the Crab-tree than I can persuade myself to feel, a work has been published, entitled, *The Legend of Shakspere's Crab-tree*, by C. F. Green. London, 1857.

let us now and then stop, and look back, and watch the
Autumn sunset fading behind us upon this our last walk,
as Shakspere often must have seen it; flake upon flake of
cloud burning with fire behind the Binton Hills, and casting
their rosy shadows to the far East, as if there another sun-
rise was dawning upon us instead of night.   And let us,
too, rising from Shakspere even up to higher things, remember, with some of that feeling of patriotism which so
marks his plays, that this was the land, where at Edgehill,
the first battle in the great struggle for English liberty was
fought, in—

His native county, which so brave spirits hath bred.

The Foot-Bridge at the Mill.

At Luddington

CHAPTER XI.

WARWICKSHIRE ORCHARDS AND HARVEST-HOMES.

I REMARKED in the first chapter how happy an event it was
that Shakspere should have been born in the centre of
England, amongst its pastures and its orchards. No poet
has such a love for nature as Shakspere; and it is this
deep, true love for her that ever gives him such a freshness,

and a healthy tone. Take the invocation to Ceres in the *Tempest* (act iv. scene 1):—

> Ceres, most bounteous lady, thy rich leas
> Of wheat, rye, barley, vetches, oats, and peas;
> Thy turfy mountains, where live nibbling sheep,
> And flat meads thatch'd with stover, them to keep;
> Thy banks with peonied and lilied brims,
> Which spongy April at thy 'hest betrims,
> To make cold nymphs chaste crowns; and thy broom groves,
> Whose shadow the dismissed bachelor loves.

Or his various descriptions of shepherd's life in *As You Like It*, and other plays, but especially the famous one in the Third Part of *King Henry VI.* (act ii. scene 5):—

> O God! methinks it were a happy life,
> To be no better than a homely swain;
> To sit upon a hill, as I do now,
> To carve out dials quaintly, point by point,
> Thereby to see the minutes, how they run;
> How many make the hour full complete,
> How many hours bring about the day,
> How many days will finish up the year,
> How many days a mortal man may live.
> *   *   *   *
> Ah, what a life were this! how sweet! how lovely!

I suppose no one would wish to prove from these passages that Shakspere was either a farmer or a shepherd, nothing beyond his love for nature and his knowledge of country scenes. And it is this love for nature that makes him ever paint her so faithfully and accurately; never suffering him to degenerate into any common-place or bald

epithet. Thus, in the first passage above quoted, he calls
April " spongy," and in the same play, the briars are
" toothed," not merely prickly, or sharp, as ordinary poets
would have written, but literally " toothed," with their
teeth-like fangs. The leaves with him are not merely
green, but " velvet" (*Love's Labour Lost*, act iv. scene 3),
thus giving their very texture and quality. So, again, in
the *Midsummer Night's Dream* (act iii. scene 2), the choughs
are not merely garrulous, or talkative, but " russet-
pated; " and in the same play, the bee is not " humming,"
or " busy," but " red-hipped; " or, as we find him calling it
in *All's Well that Ends Well* (act iv. scene 5), " red-tailed."
And so I could go on heaping up instances of his wonderful
faithfulness of detail in all his drawings of nature. And
rising, too, above this mere accuracy of description, let me
add, that he also saw into what has been well called " the
open secret " of the universe hid beneath each flower, and
each thing, without seeing which, all sight is blindness.

But just now, my object is to point out his allusions, not
so much to nature, as to certain country matters. Sheep-
shearing, and May-day, and Whitsuntide Festivals, and
Harvest-homes are all alluded to in his pages. Nay, many
things are spoken of, both by him and all the Elizabethan
dramatists, which can only be understood by one who
has long dwelt in the country. And here I am not

going into any descriptions of the beauty of the Midland orchards, but am in a most prosaic manner about to treat of their fruit, which may, perhaps, throw some little light on some passages in his plays. Take, for instance, the Clown's speech in the *Winter's Tale* (act iv. scene 2), " I must have saffron to colour the warden-pies." To this day, in the Warwickshire hedge-rows, the warden-pear, or " hard-warden," as it is more commonly called, still grows. It is of a dark green colour, when hanging on the tree, but, when kept, turns after Christmas to a deep yellow tinge. A peasant once gave me the following graphic description of it :—" It is a winter pear, rather long at the ' snout' end, and narrowish at the ' stuck' end." A warden-pie is, to this day, in Warwickshire, called a warden-cob, and consists merely of a warden-pear wrapped in a coat of paste, and then baked, forming a most primitive dish.

So again, too, in the Second Part of *King Henry IV.* (act v. scene 3), Davy serves Justice Shallow with " leathern-coats," or leatheran coats as they are now called, an apple peculiar to the neighbourhood of Stratford. A very old tree of this species was standing, till recently, at Weston Sands, from which other young trees have been raised. The fruit is still highly valued, possessing a fine white pulp, of a delicate acid flavour, beneath its thick, tough rind, whence it derives its name, sometimes to be met with in the more southern counties, under the forms of " leather-jacket," " buff-coat," and " russetine."

Other apples, too, mentioned in his plays, are found round Stratford. Thus, in the dialogue between Mercutio and Romeo (*Romeo and Juliet*, act ii. scene 4) :—

Mercutio.   I will bite thee by the ear for that jest.

Romeo.   Nay, good goose, bite not.

Mercutio.   Thy wit is a very bitter-sweeting ; it is a most sharp sauce.

Romeo.   And is it not well served unto a sweet goose?

This species is still grown, especially at Cleeve and Littleton, where it is now prized as a cider apple. It might, with more propriety, be called a " sweet-bitter," than its present country name of " bitter-sweet," for its flavour is at first sweet, and afterwards of a very astringent bitter. The minute allusion to its use as a sauce, which is still the case, I would note as an instance of Shakspere's observance in the commonest things.

Again, too, in the First Part of *King Henry IV.* (act iii. scene 3), we find Falstaff complaining that he is " withered like an old apple-John;" and in the Second Part (act ii. scene 4) we find two drawers thus conversing :—

First Drawer. What the devil hast thou brought there ? Apple-Johns ? Thou knowest, Sir John cannot endure an apple-John.

Second Drawer. Thou sayest true. The prince once set a dish of apple-Johns before him, and told him, there were five more Sir Johns: and, putting off his hat, said, " I will now take my leave of these six dry, round, old, withered knights."

7

This very apple which gave so much offence to Falstaff, may still be found at "Dancing" Marston; but only one tree remains, like that of the leather-coat at Weston Sands, quite prostrate with age; and another at Bishopton, but the species is fast wearing out and becoming very scarce. The fruit is red and ruddy, of good quality, and in perfection in September. The common notes upon this passage say that it is "an apple which will keep two years," the very reverse of the case, altogether missing the prince's joke, which likens Sir John to his red and ruddy namesake, which so soon becomes old and withered.

There is also, I may notice, in Warwickshire, a species of crab, called crab-John and crab-Jack, which will keep almost for years, and is used by the farmers for puddings in winter time, and also mixed with pears in making perry, being very juicy, but too sour by itself to make cider; but it must not be confounded with Shakspere's apple-John, of which Philips says :—

> Its withered rind, entrenched
> By many a furrow, aptly represents
> Decrepit age.   *Cider*, B. I.

thus corroborating the fitness of the prince's simile.*

---

* Steevens appositely quotes a passage from the *Ball*, by Chapman and Shirley :—

> "Thy man Apple-John, that looks
> As he had been a se'nnight in the straw,
> A-ripening for the market."

Again, too, in the same play (act v. scene 3) we find Shallow, in his house in Gloucestershire—only the other side of the Avon—saying to Falstaff, "You shall see mine orchard, where in an arbour we will eat a last year's pippin of mine own grafting, with a dish of carraways;" which do not, of course, mean the comfits of that name, as most of the notes say, but the carraway-russet, an apple still well known, both in the midland and southern counties, for its flavour and its good keeping qualities. So, too, in *Love's Labour's Lost* (act iv. scene 2), we meet the old pedant Holofernes talking about the "pomewater, who now hangeth like a jewel in the ear of *cœlo*, the sky, the welkin, the heaven, and anon falleth like a crab on the face of *terra*, the soil, the land, the earth;" which is, in its way, an excellent description, for the pomewater is a large apple, looking very tempting on the tree, but, in reality, excessively sour.*

And now for a few words about Warwickshire harvest-homes, when, as Shakspere says :—

> The Summer's green is girded up in sheaves,
> Borne on the bier with white and bristly beard.

Every one will remember the description in the *Winter's*

---

* Alluded to in the old ballad, *Blue Cap for Me* :—
   " Whose cheeks did resemble two roasting pomewaters."

Tale (act iv. scene 3) of the sheep-shearing supper, which,
by the way, Shakspere has most unaccountably placed,
when—

> The year's growing ancient—
> Not yet on summer's death, nor on the birth
> Of trembling winter,—

instead of at the latter end of the spring. Well, sheep
shearing suppers are out of date, but this passage—

> Fie, daughter! when my old wife liv'd, upon
> This day, she was both pantler, butler, cook;
> Both dame and servant; welcom'd all; serv'd all;
> Would sing her song, and dance her turn: now here
> At upper end o' the table, now, i' the middle,
> On his shoulder, and his: her face o' fire
> With labour; and the thing she took to quench it,
> She would to each one sip,—

might to this day stand as a description of a harvest-supper
at some of the old Warwickshire farm-houses. And at
such feasts some short snatches of the songs found in
Shakspere's plays may still be heard. Many of them turn
upon the same subject as Ophelia's, and it is rather difficult to separate the dross from the gold without injury
to the sense. In one that I have heard occur the very
lines :—

> Then up he rose, and donned his clothes,
> And dupped the chamber door.

And in answer to the entreaties of the maid, which are word for word with Ophelia's,—

> You promised me to wed;

the faithless swain replies,—

> I ne'er will wed with any one
> So easily found as you;

which is the same in sense as the lines in *Hamlet*. And in another song, touching on the same subject, the treacherous lover tells the forlorn maiden,—

> Go home to your father's garden:
>   *   *   *   *
> For there's a herb in your father's garden,
>   Some will call it rue:
> When fishes fly, and swallows dive,
>   Young men they will prove true.

It is the same sad rue, the "herb o' grace o' Sundays," which Ophelia reserves for herself. I have but little doubt that Shakspere heard many of the songs, which he has from memory transcribed into his plays, sung at wakes and festivals. "Let us cast away nothing, for we may live to have need of such a verse," he writes in *Troilus and Cressida;* and the songs that old Autolycus sings in the *Winter's Tale,* Shakspere may, perhaps, have picked up from some strolling pedlar, and improved with his own thoughts.*

---

* I subjoin, for the sake of comparison, an ordinary pedlar's song, from Munday's *Downfall of Robert Earl of Huntington* (act iii. scene 1), with

Antolycus's, in the *Winter's Tale* (act iv. scene 3). The reader will at once see how Shakspere has idealized the theme. First, for Mannday's:—

What lack ye? what lack ye?
What is it you will buy?
Any points, pins, or laces,
Any laces, points, or pins?
Fine gloves, fine glasses,
Any busks or masks,
Or any other pretty things?

Come, cheap for love, or buy for
Any coney, coney skins?   [money.
Or laces, points, or pins?
Fair maids, come choose or buy;
I have pretty poking-sticks,
And many other tricks,   [money.
Come, choose for love, or buy for

And now for Shakspere's:—

Lawn, as white as driven snow;
Cyprus, black as e'er was crow;
Gloves, as sweet as damask roses;
Masks for faces, and for noses;
Bugle-bracelet, necklace-amber,
Perfume for a lady's chamber;

Golden quoifs, and stomachers,
For my lads to give their dears;
Pins and poking-sticks of steel;
What maids lack from head to heel,
Come buy of me, come: come buy,
   come buy;
Buy, lads, or else your lasses cry.

What a difference there is even in the very rhythm of the lines?

Apple Gathering.

The House in Henley Street as Restored

CHAPTER XII.

THE PROVINCIALISMS OF SHAKSPERE.[*]

IT would have been singular that Shakspere, being born in Warwickshire, should not have used some of its pro-

* Some small portion of the matter in this chapter, and more in the Appendix, has appeared in a paper I contributed to *Fraser's Magazine* for October, 1856, and which the kindness of the editor has enabled me to use again. It has, however, all been entirely rewritten, and may be considered

vincialisms, or made some allusions to his native county.
I have pointed out a few of the latter in some of the
preceding pages ; but this chapter I will devote to some
of the more striking phrases found in his plays, and which
are still to be heard in the mouths of the Warwickshire
peasantry, who, now more than anybody else,

> Speak the tongue
> That Shakspere spake.

If Shakspere's own style and manner, which is undoubtedly
the case, has had a marked influence on subsequent writers,
and even on the English language itself, still his native
county left some traces of its dialect even upon him.

Johnson, himself born in a neighbouring county, first
pointed out that the expression " a mankind witch," in
the *Winter's Tale* (act ii. scene 3), was a phrase in the
Midland counties for a violent woman. And Malone, too,
showed that the singular expression in the *Tempest* (act i.
scene 2), " we cannot miss him," for, " we must not miss
him," was a provincialism of the same district. I do not
wish in any way to dogmatize on the subject, or to affirm
that the following phrases and expressions are to be found

as quite new, both in form and by additions in substance.   And here let me
take the opportunity of thanking my friend Mr. R. F. Tomes, for the great
assistance he has given me in this chapter, and without which it would
never have been written.

nowhere else but in Shakspere or Warwickshire. But it is, though, interesting to know, as was shown in a previous chapter, that the Warwickshire girls still speak of their "long purples," and "love-in-idleness;" and that the Warwickshire boys have not forgotten their "dead-men's fingers;" and that the "nine men's morris" is still played on the corn-bins of the Warwickshire farm stables, and still scored upon the greensward; and that Queen Titania would not have now to complain, as she did in the *Midsummer Night's Dream*, that it was choked up with mud; and that "Master Slender" would find his shovel-board still marked on many a public-house table and window-sill; and that he and "Master Fenton," and "good Master Brook," would, if now alive, hear themselves still so called.

Take now, for instance, the word "deck," which is so common throughout the Midland counties for a pack of cards, but in Warwickshire is often restricted to the sense of a "hand" of cards, and which gives a far better interpretation to Gloster's speech in the Third Part of *King Henry VI.* (act v. scene 1):—

> Alas, that Warwick had no more forecast,
> But whiles he thought to steal the single ten,
> The king was slyly fingered from the deck:

as, of course, there might be more kings than one in the pack, but not necessarily so in the hand. The word

" forecast," too, both as verb and noun, I might notice as being very common throughout both Warwickshire and the neighbouring counties.*

Again, in Autolycus's song, in the *Winter's Tale* (act iv. scene 2):—

> The white sheet bleaching on the hedge,
>> With heigh! the sweet birds, oh, how they sing,
> Doth set my pugging-tooth on edge,
>> For a quart of ale is dish for a king.

All the commentators here explain " pugging-tooth " as a thievish tooth, an explanation which certainly itself requires to be explained ; but most Warwickshire country people could tell them that pugging-tooth was the same as pegging or peg-tooth, that is, the canine or dog-tooth. " The child has not its pegging-teeth yet," old women still say. And thus all the difficulty as to the meaning is at once cleared.

But there is an expression used both by Shakspere and his contemporaries, which must not be so quickly passed over. Wherever there has been an unusual disturbance or ado—for I prefer using plain country words to explain others—the lower orders round Stratford-on-Avon invariably characterize it by the phrase, " there has been

---

* This word " forecast " is also used by Spenser, and others of Shakspere's contemporaries ; and, though obsolete, except amongst the peasantry of the midland districts, is, I perceive, still employed by the best American authors.

old work to-day," which well interprets the porter's allusion in *Macbeth* (act iii. scene 3), "If a man were porter
of hell-gate, he should have old turning the key," which is
simply explained in the notes as "frequent," but which
means, far more. So, in the *Merchant of Venice* (act iv.
scene 2), Portia says, "We shall have old swearing," that
is, very hard swearing; and in the *Merry Wives of Windsor*
(act i. scene 4), we find, "Here will be an old abusing of
God's patience, and the king's English;" and in the Second
Part of *King Henry IV.* (act ii. scene 4), "By the mass,
here will be old utis." And so also, in *Much Ado About
Nothing* (act v. scene 2), Ursula says, "Madam, you
must come to your uncle; yonder's old coil at home:" and
to this day, round Stratford, is this use of "old" still kept
up by the lower classes.

Again, there is another expression very common in
Warwickshire, of "being in a person's book," which must
not be confounded with the modern phrase of "being in a
person's good book." The common people always still use
the phrase without the qualifying epithet. Thus, in the
Taming of the Shrew (act ii. scene 1), in the bantering
scene between Kate and her lover, Petruchio jestingly
says, in reply to her observation that he has no arms,
"A herald, Kate? Oh! put me in thy books." So also, in
Much Ado About Nothing (act i. scene 1), the messenger

says to Beatrice, " I see the gentleman is not in your good
books ;" to which she replies, " No, an he were, I would
burn my study." The phrase, no doubt, had its origin in
servants and retainers being entered in their employers'
books, and still in Warwickshire continues in its primitive
sense.

To go on to other matters. Nothing seems to have
escaped Shakspere's eye, he drew his metaphors from all
sources. The man breaking stones in some Warwickshire by-lane would probably be able to throw some light
on this passage from the *Merchant of Venice* (act v.
scene 1) :—

> Why, this is like the mending of highways,
> In summer, when the ways are fair enough.

He would tell you that in Warwickshire, on the cold, wet
lias land, there are many roads which are scarcely passable
in winter, and are called, to this day, " summer roads ; " and
he would further add, in explanation of the passage, that
the country practice of road repairing is to draw heaps of
stone on the wayside in summer, which are only made
use of in winter; and he would further tell you the meaning of the Duke of Bourbon's speech, in *King Henry V.*
(act iii. scene 5) :—

> I will sell my dukedom,
> To buy a slobberly and a dirty farm:

and that " slobberly," or " slobbery," * is to this day applied
to the wet, dirty, Warwickshire by-roads. The house-
wife, too, at some old Warwickshire farm, with its moss-
thatched roof, will tell you that the expression in the
Taming of the Shrew (act v. scene 1), "my cake is dough,"
or, as Grumio has it in the same play, " our cake is dough
on both sides," is a common country proverb, and may be
heard any day ; † and that he who wrote,

> Sorrow concealed, like an oven stopp'd,
> Doth burn the heart to cinders where it is.

was well acquainted with country usages ;—and she will
show you the great oblong oven of former days, with its
" stopless " or " ditless," that is, the lid with which it is
stopped. But so it is with Shakspere, every trade and
calling he seems intuitively to understand. As he himself

---

* Used also in Northamptonshire. See Miss Baker's *Glossary of Northamptonshire Words.* It would, however, I feel certain, be quite unknown in
this application in many counties ; for instance, on the eocene formations
of Hampshire or Middlesex.

† How fond Shakspere was of common proverbs, the following instances
will show:—" Good wine needs no bush," *As You Like It,* in the Epilogue.
" Good liquor will make a cat speak," *The Tempest,* act i. scene 2. " Dead
as a door nail," Second Part of *King Henry IV.,* act v. scene 3. Pistol
pours them out one after the other: " Pitch and pay," " Trust no one,"
" Hold-fast is the only dog," *King Henry V.,* act ii. scene 3. So, too,
in the *Comedy of Errors,* act iii. scene 1, we find " as mad as a buck; "
and in *Much Ado About Nothing,* act ii. scene 1, " God sends a curst cow
short horns."

says, " Every lane's end, every shop, church session,
hanging, yields a careful man work." His mind readily
apprenticed itself to whatever he saw. Allusions to a
thousand occupations abound throughout his plays. For
instance, take the following : " A wit of cheverill that
stretches from an inch narrow to an ell broad." " A fish
hangs in the net like a poor man's right in the law ; 'twill
hardly come out." " A plague of opinion! a man may
wear it on both sides, like a leather jerkin." " Ignorance
is a plummet over me : " and the inference to be drawn is
not that Shakspere was a glover, or fisherman, or carpenter, but that his mind comprehended everything that
it saw. For, looking at Shakspere as a whole, we find in
him every quality that is required in any station of life.
As far as we can judge from his writings, he had the
requisites that would make a good general, a farmer, a
merchant, or a naturalist—in fact, have given him pre-
eminence in any calling. It is this manysidedness of his
that has caused all the absurd books to be written proving
that he must have been a lawyer, because he knew law so
well ; or a doctor, because he so accurately describes the
phases of certain diseases. The writers might just as well
have argued, that because Shakspere has so faithfully
described madness, that he must have been a lunatic. But
a great poet, in fact, possesses all the faculties of the rest

of the world. Shakspere's contemporary, Greene, was quite right when, in his *Groat's Worth of Wit*, he called him "an absolute Johannes Fac-totum." In anger, as well as in wine, truth is spoken.

And now, after this digression, let us return to some more provincialisms. There is a curious phrase about Stratford of "prick-eared," which I have heard nowhere else, and is now applied not so much to an abusive as to a pert and upstart person. Thus, Pistol to Corporal Nym in *King Henry V.* (act ii. scene 1): "Pish for thee, Iceland dog; thou prick-eared cur of Iceland." The metaphor has most probably been borrowed from the stable rather than the kennel, and alludes to the sharp-pointed, upright ears which some horses are continually pricking up, and in reference to this I have often heard the word used.

To proceed, a common Warwickshire expression to denote great length of time, is to say, "I have been employed here, man and boy, so many years;" so in the grave-digging scene in *Hamlet*, the sexton says of himself, "I have been sexton here, man and boy, thirty years." And in the same scene occurs another provincialism, "Make her grave straight," which Dr. Johnson imagined alluded to some particular shape, but simply means, make it quickly; just as, in the same play, Polonius says, "He will come straight," that is, immediately.

Again, a peculiar use of the verb "quoth" is noticeable among the lower orders in Warwickshire. It is universally applied to inanimate things: for instance, though the ploughshare could not speak, still the verb quoth would not be inapplicable to it. " Jerk, quoth the ploughshare," that is, the ploughshare went—to use a vulgarism—jerk. So, precisely in this sense in *Romeo and Juliet* (act i. scene 3), the old nurse says, " Shake, quoth the dove-house," that is, the dovehouse went or began shaking. Again, there is a peculiar use of the personal pronoun in Warwickshire, which I cannot do better than illustrate from Shakspere himself. Thus, in *Romeo and Juliet* (act ii. scene 4), Mercutio says of Tybalt, " He rests me his minim rest ; " and Hotspur, in the First Part of *King Henry IV.* (act iii. scene 1), thus speaks :—

> See how this river comes me, cranking in,
> And cuts me, from the best of all my land,
> A huge half-moon, a monstrous cantle out.

The punctuation is my own. The ordinary readings have no comma after " me," in the first line, though they insert it after the " me " in the second. Mortimer immediately after uses the same phrase, though not so strongly marked. So also Falstaff says, in praise of good sherris-sack, in the Second Part of *King Henry IV.* (act iv. scene 3), " It ascends me into the brain, dries me there all the foolish, and dull, and crudy vapours." So also again, in *Troilus and Cressida* (act i. scene 2), perhaps the strongest instance of all, Pandarus thus describes the love of Helen for Troilus: "She came, and puts me her white hand to his cloven chin." Such a phrase can hardly well be explained. Those who have been in the habit of mixing with the common people of Warwickshire will at once recognize it as quite familiar to their ears.

The number of words used in Shakspere's plays now heard only in the Midland counties, and which can there be better explained than by any learned commentary, is, to say the least, curious. To confine ourselves to Warwickshire — there is the expressive compound "bloodboltered" in *Macbeth* (act iv. scene 1), which the critics have all thought meant simply blood-stained. Miss Baker, in her *Glossary of Northamptonshire Words*, first pointed out that "bolter" was peculiarly a Warwickshire word, signifying to clot, collect, or cake, as snow does in a horse's hoof, thus giving the phrase a far greater intensity of meaning. And Steevens, too, first noticed, that in the expression in the *Winter's Tale* (act iii. scene 3), " Is it a boy or a child ?"—where, by the way, every actor tries to make a point, and the audience invariably laughs—that the word " child " is used, as is sometimes the case in the midland districts, as synonymous with girl ; which is plainly

its meaning in this passage, although the speaker has used
it just before in its more common sense of either a boy or
a girl.

Again, there is the word " gull," in *Timon of Athens*
(act ii. scene 1),

> But I do fear,
> When every feather sticks in his own wing,
> Lord Timon will be left a naked gull,
> Which flashes now a phœnix;

which most of the critics have thought alluded to a sea-
gull, whereas it means an unfledged nestling, which to this
day is so called in Warwickshire.   And this interpretation
throws a light on a passage in the First Part of *King
Henry IV.* (act v. scene 1):—

> You used me so,
> As that ungentle gull, the cuckoo's bird,
> Useth the sparrow;—

where some notes amusingly say that the word alludes
to the voracity of the cuckoo.   I may add that the Warwickshire farmers' wives even now call their young gos-
lings gulls.

There is also a very common Warwickshire phrase,
" contain yourself," that is, restrain yourself; and so in
Timon of Athens (act ii. sc. 2), Timon says to his creditor's
servant, " Contain yourself, good friend;" and so again,
in *Troilus and Cressida* (act v. sc. 2), Ulysses says:—

> O contain yourself,
> Your passion draws ears hither.

And in the *Two Gentlemen of Verona* (act iv. scene 4), we find Launce using the still rarer phrase of " keep your-self," in the same sense to his dog Crab.

I will not, though, dwell too long upon a subject which, however curious, is still of very secondary importance. For the benefit of those who take an interest in word-lore, I have ventured to give in an Appendix a short glossary of words used in Shakspere's plays which are still to be heard in Warwickshire. For it is, after all, touching to think that, amidst the change that is ever going on, the same phrases which Shakspere spoke are still spoken in his native county, and that the flowers are still called by the same names which he called them.

Honey Stalks

CHAPTER XIII.

SHAKSPERE.

I should indeed be guilty of giving *Hamlet* without Hamlet, were I to omit a chapter upon Shakspere himself, for I will not pay so bad a compliment to the reader as to suppose that he is impelled by the mere love of vulgar sight-seeing to visit Stratford. And my aim here will be, what it has been throughout the book, to show Shakspere as a moralist, and to remove the impression of that common opinion about him, which is still so current, that he was a great irregular genius. And let no one take alarm at that word moralist, for by it I simply wish to indicate the comprehensive manner in which Shakspere ought to be treated. I am not going to prove that he belonged to any school or sect, but simply intend treating him as the Catholic priest of all humanity, believing with Milton that " the lofty grave tragedians are the teachers best of moral prudence." The word " moralist" includes everything concerning a man; and no great work of art can help but be deeply moral, for the insight into the Beautiful is the insight into the Divine, and the artist, to see the Beautiful, must necessarily be imbued with reverence and religion. This is an old truth, too often in our days forgotten; Strabo affirmed it in a passage before quoted; ἡ ἀρετὴ ποιητοῦ συνέζευκται τῇ τοῦ ἀνθρώπου, καὶ οὐκ οἰόντε ἀγαθὸν γενέσθαι ποιητὴν, μὴ πρότερον γενηθέντα ἄνδρα ἀγαθόν. And Milton said the same, when he declared that the writer of a poem must himself be a perfect poem.

But in the case of Shakspere we are too likely to over-look the point. His great command and power of language, his gorgeous colouring, and his imagery attract most readers to their superficial beauty, instead of directing them to the inner unity of the piece. His plays are so composite, so filled with both variety of character and matter, that we are in danger of losing sight of the simple idea round which everything moves. Hence he has been accused of writing without plan, or moral purpose. Even Wordsworth says,—

> We must be free or die, who speak the *tongue*
> That Shakspere spake, *the faith and morals hold*
> Which Milton held.

And the same vicious distinction is made, if not by our best, by our most popular critics.

Another reason for this view is that Shakspere has no definite system, no special morality; he is too sound to bring into prominence any one article, or creed, at the expense of another. He is like Nature: the trees and the flowers in Nature silently blossom, and bloom alike in open places and wildest desert, and to the common mind they have no meaning. They say never a word, and yet are full of meaning. The world moves on, and in silence the seasons come and go, and leave no impression on the ordinary man; yet who shall say they teach no lesson? The gloom of the mountains, the brightness of the valleys, the sunshine clothing wold and wood, the sternness of winter, the joy of spring, are all full of meaning.

In speaking, therefore, of Shakspere as a moralist, I repeat that my wish is to include him under the widest possible term ; for morality, as was before said, includes everything in a man. A man's intellect is nothing else but the vital force within him, speaking more or less distinctly. His deeds, his words, his writings, his very expression of face are the outcome of that moral force. You cannot separate the moral from the intellectual man. Hence a man's writings contain the best history of his inner life, in fact, of himself; they cannot speak falsely of him. When I read these lines,—

> The floor of heaven
> Is thick inlaid with patines of bright gold ;
> There's not the smallest orb, which thou behold'st
> But in his motion like an angel sings,
> Still quiring to the young-eyed cherubim:
> Such harmony is in immortal souls;
> But whilst this muddy vesture of decay
> Doth grossly close it in, we cannot hear it,—

I feel that Shakspere was a good man, because to the bad the secrets of Nature can never be revealed. The bad man cannot possibly report Nature's inner spirit, any more than a man born blind can, from his own knowledge, describe a rainbow : let me repeat, as emphatically as I can, that a bad man can only see the outside of Nature, and that not in its own pure light, but coloured by his own

diseased vision. He can never sink any deep shafts into
Nature, and extract the riches and the golden wealth of
contentment, with which she rewards her true lovers and
worshippers. Such a passage as that quoted above, settles
the question of the general tenour of Shakspere's life. I
can no more believe the common tradition about his being
a loose liver, than I can Homer's blindness. I do not
for one moment mean to say that Shakspere never fell into
temptation. He was, as far as we can judge, a man above
all others whose nature was so sensitively framed as to
receive an impression from all objects, and on this account
must have been above all others scourged with the penalties
of our humanity. He most of all must have been stretched
upon the rack of the senses. No doubt, like the poet-king
of Israel he was often vanquished by the outer world, but
only for a time; and depend also upon this, that every time
that he fell, by so much was the strength of his intellect
weakened, and his sight grew dim, and his gift of language
palsied. Hence, too, that other popular idea of his passing
through the world without care or trouble, is equally foolish.
A good life is the development of God within us, but
developed only by one long series of battles and wrestlings
against evil. When I read *Hamlet*, and *Lear*, and *Othello*,
I wonder that writing them had not made Shakspere
" lean," as Dante said of himself. And so they would

had not Shakspere possessed that wondrous, gentle, loving spirit of a child, melting the cares that must have lain round his heart.

And if I were asked to mention what one particular trait I found most conspicuous in Shakspere, I should answer, —not his imagination, not his power of language, great as these were, but this very Love. He seems to have loved each thing; and this spirit of love bathes everything he touches in its joy and sunshine. I cannot separate the name of Shakspere from the idea of love. There is a proverb Mr. Carlyle is fond of quoting, that "love furthers knowledge," and it is in Shakspere's case most true. Shakspere in reality sees both deeper and wider with the heart than the intellect, and *ubi charitas ibi claritas*, says a still older proverb. All his judgments of men and things are made with a reference to this charity of love; he seems almost to solve the enigma of life by love. Love, it might almost be said, takes with him the place of duty; his plays overflow with the spirit of kindness and gentleness; his heroines— "Shakspere's women," as a poet has since called them— make life and love synonymous. His heroes, had they gone to battle, might all of them have carried on their shields the simple motto "Amo," borne by the good knight of old. And theirs and Shakspere's love is not ordinary love, but that love without which life and the world cannot

be understood, without which, in fact, there is no knowledge.

And so, too, no difficulty exists in accounting for the profound bitterness with which Shakspere sometimes looks on
life. It is but this love speaking in its earnestness. The
most loving souls have in them, above all others, the capacity
for scorn in its bitterest intensity. Plato notices that
comedy and tragedy are more closely united than might
at first sight be supposed, and are ever to be found in the
same poet. So too the intensest love and the intensest bitterness may be found in the same soul. For
that bitterness is but the converse of that love ; so, therefore, we need not be surprised at finding the man who can
so lovingly draw his fellow-creatures in their common
everyday pursuits of life, girding at " the fool multitude
that choose by show," calling them " the many-headed
beast," " who if they love they know not why, they hate
for no better reason ; " because he, knowing so well the
preciousness of that love, which never swerves, knows
also how miserably vile are those who have flung it away.
Again, too, from this cause, the man who above all others
prizes the sweets of love and friendship, the joys of childhood, of fatherhood, of brotherly and sisterly affection,
can, when these are all gone, find nothing to value, and
must vent his scorn in the misanthropy of some Timon.

He believes, as Plato has well put it, in human virtue, in human love, in noble feelings, but by some sudden wrench his friends prove faithless, his ideal dream is broken, and he wakes up in a cold, barren world, and his love is soured into poison. So, too, will this very love, that so dotes upon the beauties of the plains and the woodlands, and the whole moving pageant of Nature, exclaim in the dark night of its terrible reaction of grief and bitterness of heart, " that this goodly frame, the earth, is a sterile promontory; this most excellent canopy the air, this brave overhanging firmament, this majestical roof fretted with golden fire, appear no other than a foul pestilent congregation of vapours." But this is a mood which only lasts for a short time with Shakspere; love again with him soon resumes its old sway, and colours all things with deepest joy and gladness.

This love, too, singular though it may at first appear, gives Shakspere his peculiar humour. If, as Goethe has well remarked, nothing is so characteristic of a person as what each finds to be laughable, so, also, nothing is so characteristic of an author as the style of his wit and humour. Shakspere's humour differs very widely from that of the mere satirist, who too often does but little good to the reader, and always positive harm to himself. There is not only breadth, but depth, in the

humour of Shakspere. His is not the laughter for mere
laughter's sake. It is difficult to define anything, but
more especially humour, which is rather than anything
else a feeling of the heart, steeping everything in its own
warm, mellow sunshine of love. This is the humour of
Shakspere, a loving, sympathetic humour, drawing upon
humanity itself for its themes, sometimes indeed sad, but
never tinged with any levity or heartlessness. Once
or twice, perhaps, he may touch upon topics which are
not fit subjects for mirth, but this arises from dramatic
necessity, rather than from any other cause. Take, though,
as a whole, all his humourists, and we shall find that they
leave us merrier and wiser. There is Falstaff, who "can
teach twenty men, but who cannot take one man's advice,"
whose death-bed scene is dwelt upon with a charity that
should make us remember we are no fit judges of our
brother's faults. There are all the clowns, too, from
the clown in the *Winter's Tale,* who was "a gentleman
born before his father," and to prove the fact, thought
it incumbent to swear, up to Launce, whose very dog
has more humour than most human beings. And then,
rising from these up to such moralists as Touchstone,
who takes for his text, "The fool doth think he is wise,
but the wise man knows himself to be a fool;" and the
Jester in *Lear,* whose end of life is but "going to bed

at noon," we may through them better understand life
itself. Shakspere's humour is essentially what Schiller
would have called " *Spieltrieb*." Without it life can never
be seen ; for humour looks upon life with a sort of earnest
sport, its playfulness tinging its seriousness. It is not
merely negative, as some have said, or else it would
sink to mere wit; nor, like wit, does it deal with the
fleeting, external affinities of things, but sees into their
deeper relationships. Take, as an example, the Induction
to the *Taming of the Shrew*, the centre of which is life
viewed by a drunken clown ; or Gonzalo's model Utopia
in the *Tempest;* or the nephelococcygia of Jack Cade
in the Second Part of *King Henry VI.;* or, better still,
the grave-digging scene in *Hamlet*. In all of these,
but especially in the last, we find the deepest and sternest
relations of life touched upon, and a new light thrown
upon them.

Let me now also notice what may appear slight
and trivial to some, Shakspere's love for children and
childhood. There is a healthiness and a joy about
it which should not be passed over. I am not speaking now of the higher love which he always represents
— a father feeling for his child, or a child for its
parent, but that happy view of children and child's
life that he paints. Take, for instance, how Polixenes,

in the *Winter's Tale* (act i. scene 1), describes his boy, as :—

> All my exercise, my mirth, my matter,
> Now my sworn friend, and then mine enemy:
> My parasite, my soldier, statesman, all:
> He makes a July's day, short as December.

Or, again, look at the scene in the next act between Mamillius and his mother, where the little rogue tries to frighten her by beginning so solemnly, "There was a man dwelt by a churchyard." This joyful way in which Shakspere touches upon children is very beautiful. For one more illustration, take Valeria's description, in *Coriolanus* (act i. scene 3), of Virgilia's boy, who "ran after a gilded butterfly, and when he caught it, he let it go again; and after it again; and over and over he comes, and up again, and caught it again:" a picture which is very natural. I make no apology for dwelling upon this subject, so likely from its apparent triviality to be overlooked, but none the less important, as showing Shakspere's healthy tone of mind.

Nor let us forget the higher love which Shakspere ever draws of a father feeling for his son, or a child for its parents. In the speech of Ulysses, in *Troilus and Cressida* (act i. scene 3), the height of civil discord is marked by a son striking his father. The most touching scene in *Coriolanus* is where the Roman general, well knowing that he shall have to pay the price of death for his affection, yet ungrudgingly gives his love to his mother. She conquers when all Rome failed. In *King Lear* filial love is the organic centre round which all turns. So, also, in the abstract, is old age venerable, loveable, in Shakspere's eyes. The greatest fault that Ulysses can find in Achilles is that he should laugh at Nestor, and that "the faint defects of age" should be turned into ridicule. All this is very beautiful, showing how thoroughly Shakspere felt life to be sublime.

Again, too, the proverb, "love furthers knowledge," holds good in his descriptions of natural scenery. I have in a previous chapter spoken of this love for nature, but I cannot possibly dwell too much upon it in these days of overgrown towns, and smoke, and din, and factories. As was before said, this true love for nature, almost rising into an affection as for a personal human being, makes him know her so well, and describe her so accurately. We find it even in his very earliest pieces. Take, for instance, that description in the *Venus and Adonis*—

> The studded bridle on a ragged bough
> Nimbly she fastens:

what beauty there is in that epithet "ragged"—that

is, ragged with bits and fragments of gray moss.   Take
another picture, in *As You Like It* (act iv. scene 3), of
a similar scene :—

> An oak, whose boughs were mossed with age,
> And high top bald with dry antiquity.

Shakspere paints his pictures as accurately as nature does,
leaving nothing unfinished, no line hurried or blurred ;
feeling that, above all, " truth is truest poesy." For instance, examine the following lines from *Cymbeline* (act iv.
scene 2) :—

> With fairest flowers
> While summer lasts, and I live here, Fidele,
> I'll sweeten thy sad grave; thou shalt not lack
> The flower, that's like thy face, pale primrose; nor
> The azur'd harebell, like thy veins; no, nor
> The leaf of eglantine, whom, not to slander,
> Outsweeten'd not thy breath: the ruddock would,
> With charitable bill (oh! bill, sore shaming
> Those rich-left heirs, that let their fathers lie
> Without a monument!), bring thee all this;
> Yea, and furr'd moss beside, when flowers are none,
> To winter-ground thy corse.

Analyze the whole piece, mark first the mention of the
primroses, because they come first, pale as Imogen's face,
reminding us of the passage in the *Winter's Tale*—" pale
primroses that die unmarried." And then, too, notice the
harebell, that is, the hyacinth of spring, the common bluebell, which we saw in such quantities in the woods round

Stratford, and which blooms somewhat later than the primrose, in whose blue he can see nothing less beautiful than Imogen's veins. And then mark, too, he mentions the leaf of the eglantine, that is, the sweet-briar—not its flower, which has not yet blossomed, but the leaf, which, when rubbed in the hands, is so very sweet. And lastly, too, notice that beautiful epithet " furred " applied to the moss, giving us its very texture.

Even his love for colour does not lead Shakspere into mistakes: take the lines in *Timon of Athens* (act iv. scene 3):—

> The black toad, and adder blue,
> And gilded newt.

The toad is here black, because, by being spotted with black, and by its ugliness and its supposed evil qualities, it becomes to the imagination really black; and the adder is blue, although only the under part is a dull blue; but because by this we can most readily distinguish it from the common harmless snake, he calls it generally blue, although only one portion is so. And the newt is gilded, not only from its yellow colour, but because it is so fond of basking in the warm sunshine, which makes it seem golden.

But Shakspere's love for nature does not stop here. He clearly sees that drawing nature accurately is not

9

the only thing necessary—perhaps by itself is valueless,
unless he can connect nature with life, and by her explain
its mysteries. He therefore uses her forms as a language,
and she becomes in his hands an interpreter between us
and the invisible world. All her shapes and emblems
are to him an alphabet by which he may read "the
open secret" of the universe. Here lies the real difference between the true poet and the impostor. For
no man, except the pure in spirit, can have this insight,
this divination into nature, for she also is pure, and all
things can be but interpreted by the same spirit as that
which they are. The base man can no more understand
nature than a deaf man the music of Beethoven. He
not only cannot now, but it is impossible for him ever
to do so, try how he may, as long as he is at all base.
Shakspere, by his pure, deep love, pierced below the
surface of things, and saw there the divine spirit of life.
In this sense Novalis's saying about Shakspere is to be
understood, that "his dramas are products of nature, as
deep as nature herself." And this is wonderfully true,
for the greatest man may be known by this sign, that
he is most in unison with nature, that he allies his poetry
with her own, and by her help explains the mysteries
and wonders within our souls. Nature herself is the
greatest poet, and the pure, reverent soul draws its

inspiration from her, receiving for its blessing and its precious reward, that it is more and more taken into her bosom.

Of course I do not mean to say that love, in its usual sense, as well as in its higher meanings of charity and sympathy, is the only key to Shakspere's mind. Yet still I do think that it is the most conspicuous trait in his writings. This gives him that spirit of forbearance, the characteristic of every noble mind, which made him exclaim more than once, "Judge not, for we are sinners all." This makes him draw real men and women with human affections and human sympathy, never scorning the poorest or the lowest. From his plays may be compiled a litany of precious thoughts, of which charity is the basis, teaching us how that ever "the rarer action is in virtue than in vengeance," that we should "cherish those hearts that hate us," and that we should let "gentleness our strong enforcement be." He sympathizes with everything, not only with man, but the poor beetle and the worm that we tread upon. And in his plays we are ever meeting with that spirit, which found its fullest expression in Wordsworth's lines—

Never to blend our pleasure, or our pride,
With sorrow of the meanest thing that feels.

More upon this subject of loving charity I shall have to

say when I mention Shakspere's religious opinions. Now let us turn to other characteristics. And first of all, of his patriotism, which is something more than the mere outcome of dramatic character. In his pages we find reflected all the spirit and chivalry of one of the noblest eras of English history. His patriotism literally burns in his lines. He seems to have had that same feeling which made Homer say, " The one best omen is to fight for fatherland." His is not the mere vaporous rant of a charlatan, nor the adroitness of a party statesman trying to make political capital, but the true, deep love of the patriot, glorying in the nobleness and high-mindedness of his country, and feeling beyond all bitterly pained when she stoops to what is mean and base. This is the key-note to all his historical plays. He dearly loves that " sea-walled isle," that " pale, that white-faced shore," which in another place he so lovingly describes as—

This precious stone set in a silver sea.

It is this patriotism that makes him in *King John* exclaim—

Nought shall make us rue
If England to herself do rest but true.

In which lines, perhaps, are included all that a statesman need require to govern his country. It is certainly well worth reflecting how dearly Shakspere loved his country, in these days of ours, when there are men who would about as much dream of defending it as rabbits their burrows. Yet, on the other hand, has Shakspere, more eloquently than any Peace Society, painted the horrors of war in that one terrible cartoon of—

> Mars, at whose heels,
> Leashed in like hounds, should famine, sword, and fire
> Crouch for employment ;

and denounced as criminal the passion for war—war which Othello so bitterly says " makes ambition virtue."

Let me now notice, for it is most important, how true an artist Shakspere was. No vicious incident, no strained effect at the cost of virtue, no unnatural situation, disfigure his pages, to catch any temporary applause. He gave no " sweet, sweet poison for the age's tooth." Beaumont and Fletcher were, for reasons which eternally redound to Shakspere's credit, the favourites on the stage after his death. Truly great was he that he respected not the suffrages of the " groundlings." He cared not " to set on some quantity of barren spectators to laugh." He minded not the applause of " the youths that thunder at a playhouse," nor of those who come merely to hear—

> A noise of targets, or to see a fellow
> In a long motley coat, guarded with yellow.

These and such as these he tells us will be disappointed

with him and his plays.   He is evidently the true artist
who loves his work, and will not allow it to be spoilt by
one single word or letter, for the fleeting caprice of the
moment.   There was nothing about him of the spirit of
Lope de Vega, who, to gain popularity, acknowledged that
he pandered to the tastes of his audience and his age.
Shakspere wrote, not as if clownish boys, but real Cordelias
and Imogens performed their own parts on the stage.
And it was this moral delicacy of taste—and taste, be it
observed, is not an acquirement, but the outcome of a pure
soul—that made him in *King John* humanize the spirit of
the older drama, and in *Hamlet* refine the coarse features
of the Ophelia of the original story, and in the *Merchant of
Venice* fling away the dross, and keep only the gold of the
old play.

I have spoken of the joy that pervades Shakspere: still
there is another side of his nature to be looked at; and
we cannot but feel the somewhat cold, stern view of life
that he takes.   This arises from his greatness; he is ever
unmoved; sunshine and shadow play alternately across his
scenes, and we know not with which he sympathizes.   Good
and evil come and go, and he seems not to mind.   His
great nature takes all in, as the sea does alike the Amazons,
or the mountain rill, or the filthy drain, purifying them
all in its vast alembic.   And in his later plays, too, a some-

what bitter tone of feeling is perhaps observable, as if when the sun of his life was setting, some dark clouds rose and gathered round it, not untinged, though, with light and hope. But we must remember that sorrow and even bitterness of soul are proportioned to a man's greatness, and it is as true now as ever, that increase of knowledge increaseth sorrow. Walpole said, " Life is a tragedy to those who feel, a comedy to those who think." It is a comedy to no one but the fool; the lesson of life is like the lesson of history—though full of hope, still very sad ; and tragic poetry is the record of our deepest griefs, of the struggles of our better nature with the brute within us ; the tale of our free-will, according to our strength or our weaknesses, either proving itself victorious over, or yielding to, necessity; a tragedy itself which is enacted either successfully or not by every one who lives.

Perhaps from his occasionally stern view of life has arisen the accusation that Shakspere does not make virtue triumphant. It is a pitiful charge, and whoso expects his good actions to be rewarded, deserves whatever ill may befall him. It is only a platitude to say that virtue is its own reward, and yet men never seem to realize its truth. What Shakspere teaches is what every high-minded man would teach, that rewards are the last things the good themselves expect.

Yet notwithstanding this view of life, as seen at times in the action and development of his plays; notwithstanding, too, his many bitter outbursts against Fortune, Shakspere is constantly dwelling upon the power of man over circumstances, and the triumph of man's free-will over necessity. " Give me the man who is not passion's slave," is the continual cry of his soul, so unlike the creed of his brother dramatist, who held that " we ne'er are angels till our passions die." It is not the absence of passion, but its subjection, that gives man the ultimate victory.

> To thine ownself be true,
> And it must follow, as the night the day,
> Thou canst not then be false to any one,—

is not the mere speaker's creed, but the doctrine that runs through the whole of Shakspere's plays. Whatever else may be said of *Coriolanus* as a whole, and doubtless there is much, yet one of the greatest lessons of that play is to show how a great man is self-subsistent; his enemies cannot persecute him; banishment to him is impossible. " I banish you," says Coriolanus; " not you, me. There is a world elsewhere," besides at Rome. You can rob me of hearth and fire, and some few yards of roof-shelter, but that is all. A man is not the creature of circumstances; they in no ways affect him; but he moulds them. The true man is, as the guards say of Menenius, " the oak not to be windshaken ; " or, as Coriolanus better puts it, " extremity is the trier of spirits." Such seems to me at least one of the morals of the play. And the same lesson is taught throughout Shakspere, that external circumstances have no power over us, that we ourselves are our worst enemies, and that from within, and not from without, harm comes; that worldly misfortunes cannot hurt us; on the contrary, if we use them rightly, may do us much good. What if they do come? " There is no time so miserable but a man may be true." " It is the mind that makes the body rich," he is constantly saying. No man ever read to the world such fine lessons from Adversity, as Shakspere. He was the first who crowned her with a precious jewel on her head: before his time she had been sister to the Furies; he made her a fourth Grace.

And now for a few words upon Shakspere's religious views; and here again his wide-world charity and love meet us. There is nothing sectarian about him; he is thoroughly catholic, shining like the sun on the good and the bad. " I'd beat him like a dog," exclaims Sir Andrew, in *Twelfth Night*. " What, for being a Puritan ? " exclaims Sir Toby, with exquisite irony. From this cause is Shakspere's Shylock so very different from the stage Jew of the time, " who was baited through five long acts." The most careless reader must perceive that the calamities which

befall Shylock arise not because he is a Jew, but a bad
man. The character too is not drawn for the mere character's sake ; most skilfully does Shakspere turn Shylock to
good account, as a means whereby to attack the shortcomings of Christians.   In no other play, and by no other
character, could this have been so well done. Through him
Shakspere denounces slavery, then lately introduced by
Sir John Hawkins into England ; through him, too, he
exposed the intolerance of the times, which made Marlowe's
Jew of Malta a popular play, and " the Jew himself, God
bless the mark, a kind of devil."

So again in this wide spirit that " one touch of Nature
makes the whole world kin," does he draw Friar Laurence
in *Romeo and Juliet*, at a time when Romanist priests were
hung at Tyburn.   And in the same spirit, when Leontes
tells Paulina that she shall be burnt, he makes her
reply,

> It is a heretic that makes the fire,
> Not she which burns in it ;

and this too when Francis Kett was being burnt for
heresy at Norwich.

Let us notice too with what reverence Shakspere ever
treats religion and religious subjects. Bacon has said,
" admiratio est semen sapientiæ." But reverence is wisdom
itself, its beginning and its end.   Against Puritanism only

SHAKSPERE.   139

does Shakspere strike; and yet, as we have above seen, there is no ill-nature in his blows. I yield to no one in my admiration of the Puritans, but there is a side of their character I cannot admire; they left quite out of view the culture of men's æsthetic nature, which is not only necessary for a right existence, but with religion, of which too it forms a part, makes up life. The higher and more deeply cultivated Puritan, like Milton, well knew this. Of the average Puritan I now only speak, who thought that because he was virtuous there should be no more cakes and ale. And in looking at Shakspere's criticism of Puritanism, we must not forget the violent attacks the Puritans had already made even in his time against the stage.

Let us notice also Shakspere's liberality in other things which were then looked upon as vitally mixed up with religion, such as his treatment of witches at a time when the King of England was writing a book upon the justice of punishing them, and when Acts of Parliament were passed, condemning to death any one concerned with so-called witchcraft. No faith had he either in the astrology of the day. He tells us, over and over again, that " men at some times are masters of their fates : the fault is not in our stars, but in ourselves."

But it is because Shakspere reflected all that was noble and good in the religion of his age, that he will live for all ages. His Protestantism was not confined to a protest against popery, but against the popery of sectarianism and narrow-mindedness of any kind. And this matter of Protestantism is far too important to be settled in a sentence. The real question is, How far, and in what way, did Protestantism affect Shakspere? I think the answer is contained in the examples just given of his thoroughly catholic treatment of all religious creeds. The end and aim of Protestantism is to emancipate the subjectivity of the mind from any objective power, and this is what is accomplished by Shakspere. This makes the difference between him and all other writers; the views of most authors are so entirely built upon some narrow creed of their own day, that they are fit only for readers of that creed, and their own day. But the true poet is for all time, and creeds, and people; and for much of his largeness and liberality of view was Shakspere undoubtedly indebted to Protestantism, into whose noble inner meaning he had strength to see.

And this question of Protestantism is so intimately mixed up with Shakspere's age, that we must look also at the age itself for a solution of Shakspere's principles. Schiller well says, "The artist is the son of his age; but pity for him if he is its pupil. The matter of his works he will take from the present, but their form he will devise from a nobler time, nay, from beyond all time, from the absolute unchanging unity of his own nature." And this is most true of Shakspere. The poet is ever the reflex of his age, giving back in his own mirror the idealized forms and thoughts of his time. Shakspere lived on the threshold of a new era. Behind him the sun of the middle ages was for ever setting, tinging everything with its bright colours, whilst before him was rising the clear white dawn of the modern spirit of inquiry. Learning and philosophical research had already arisen. The old current of the Reformation was flowing in a new direction, some day to flood the dry places of the earth, and with its waves to sweep away the English monarchy.

This must be carefully borne in mind when inquiring into Shakspere's views of life. He did not live to see the effects of this new spirit of inquiry and free thought; but he must have, in some measure, when speculating, to quote his own expressive phrase, upon

The prophetic soul
Of the wide world dreaming on things to come,--

have foreseen some of its issues. This fact, as Ulrici has shown, will reconcile so much that is else contradictory in his plays. There we find, in bare, naked contrast, the two spirits of his day—the old and the new view of the world and life, so opposite and so sharply marked; on the one hand, the objectivity of the middle ages; and on the other, the definite consciousness and the modern spirit of freedom of discussion.

From this latter arises in his plays a tendency to speculation. Hence does he preach the doctrine, that " ignorance is God's curse," and that, above all things, " thought is free ;" or, as he puts it elsewhere—

> Truth can never be confirmed enough,
> Though doubts did ever sleep.

Like all wise men, he leans trustfully on that beneficent Power, who sent us into the world. As we come here, so we must go. " Ripeness is all." And he sings of the grave, not as the prison-house of the body, but the bridal-chamber, where the soul will be mated with all that is purest and holiest.

Hence, too, from this double view of life partly arise all the contradictions in his plays. I say, partly, because every great man, in proportion to his greatness, is full of contradictions. Plato and Shakspere especially are so. And they are so, because they, more than any one else, can see and feel the contradictions and the incompleteness of the world and life itself.

But it is by contrasting Shakspere with the old Greek dramatist, that we can best see how far his views of life were affected by modern thought. With the old Greek, the black gloom of destiny enshrouded everything. The

cloud shows but a hand's breadth in size at the beginning
of the play, but keeps gradually darkening and darkening
until it bursts with all its lurid gloom and fury. With
Shakspere, man, if he can find out the right way, is at
least the arbiter of his own fate. The end and aim of man,
with Shakspere, is to reconcile the free-will of his own
mind with moral necessity ; and when man cannot do this,
when he fails, through weakness or pride, or stubbornness
of heart, then comes the true tragedy of life, miserable,
heart-rending.

The following may better explain Shakspere's theory of
free-will and destiny:—A blind girl used to read the
raised type of her Bible by her fingers. Through an ill-
ness, her power of touch lost its sensitiveness, and day by
day she felt it leaving her, until she lost it altogether.
She could no longer read her Book of Life. She was cut
off from all light. In her agony of despair, she took up
her book, as she imagined, for the last time, and kissed it ;
and, to her surprise and deep joy, the power which had
been taken away from her fingers she found still remained,
with trebled sensitiveness, on her lips. Once more she
could read. This, with Shakspere, is the case with man.
Man is blindly groping about the world, feeling his way.
By-and-by, he entirely loses the faint clue he once had.
And not until he reconciles himself with fate—as it were

kisses necessity—is he able to read and understand the
Book of Life.

All this is, after all, a poor, barren, meagre account of
Shakspere. We can no more judge of a man by a few
quotations from his works, than of the infinite grandeur of
the sea by a few buckets-full of water brought up as a
specimen. I should have liked to have analyzed a play
or two, and shown how the views that I have stated are
borne out. But this chapter has already exceeded the
limits originally intended.

Of Shakspere's personal life, as we have already seen
it is a series of conjectures. All that is known of him in
connection with Stratford has been related in previous
chapters. The little information we possess from other
sources is most valuable, especially the documents discovered by Mr. Collier amongst the papers at Bridgewater
House, with the signature of " H. S.," supposed to stand
for Henry, Earl of Southampton, addressed to the Chan-
cellor Ellesmere, on behalf of Burbage and Shakspere,
whose theatre was " threatened," to quote the expression
in the letter, by the Lord Mayor and the Aldermen of
London. The latter portion of it thus runs: ". . . their
trust and suit now is, not to be molested in their way of
life, whereby they maintain themselves, and their wives

and families (both being married, and of good reputation), as well as the widows and orphans of some of their dead fellows." This care for the orphans and widows of their friends is, indeed, touching and beautiful, and in accordance with all we know of Shakspere's character.*

The few allusions in his plays to his personal friends bear the same testimony to his goodness and gentleness of heart. Such is that in *As You Like It* (act iii. scene 5), to his poor friend Marlowe, as "the dead shepherd;" but still finer, in the *Midsummer Night's Dream*, that to Greene, in the lines,—

> The thrice three Muses mourning for the death
> Of Learning, late deceased.

Such is the epitaph he writes over the man who with his dying breath abused him. I know no other such example of truest Christian charity in all literature.

His sonnets bear the same testimony. I am amongst those who, with Schlegel, regard them as autobiographical. There is, doubtless, much that is dramatic in them, for Shakspere's genius was essentially dramatic. But allowing this its full weight, we see in them the true man revealing himself. They tell us the tale, which every one to a certain extent has felt, of friendship and love won and

---

* It is but right to say that there have been doubts thrown on this letter. But the best critics, including Mr. Halliwell, maintain its genuineness.

lost—somewhat, perhaps, hyperbolically expressed, but still, in the main, true. They tell us, too, the dark conflict of passion and perplexity, which we all, according to our natures, suffer; they show us, also, that profoundly melancholy side of the highest intellects, prone to brood on misery, which at times, from the depths of a bitter experience, so loves to paint not only its own griefs, but "dark, ideal hues;" but, above all, do they tell us the man's strong, passionate love, conquering everything else. "Love is my sin," he cries, in Sonnet CXLII.; and so all through them we find the outpourings of a spirit of love and friendship.

I know it is often said that critics discover in Shakspere's writings hidden beauties which Shakspere himself knew not; but this is far truer, that every great poet intuitively seizes upon truths, and writes them without being conscious. The great man is always greater than he knows: and at first sight, as has been said before, Shakspere appears to be entirely without purpose, as if he were appointed to simply transcribe what he saw without comment or bias of his own. The deepest moral, though, is never written in larger print: what is obvious is generally not worth much: and as with Nature so with Shakspere: the problems of life we are left to solve; and Shakspere's characters must speak to us themselves, or not at all.

And the highest power any writer can evince, is that without comment or remark, he is able to draw his characters so that the reader may love the good, and loathe the bad. And this depends upon no wire-drawn moral, or objective incident, or making virtue triumphant, but simply, as has been said long ago, upon the ἦθος τοῦ λέγοντος, the true reverential spirit, which bows itself before the mysteries of life, and impresses itself upon everything it touches, and which so thoroughly imbues Shakspere's nature. Compared with this all else is secondary, valueless.

Here I must at length stop. Briefly, let me say of Shakspere, that in him are united the excellences of all other poets that ever lived. He combines the sweetness and the lyrical power of Beaumont and Fletcher, with the wit of Jonson, and the grandeur of Milton, and the chivalry of Spenser—just as it was said that the beauty of all other women was to be found in Helen of Argos. And the greatest praise which can be given Shakspere, is to say that he is not a person, but a name. These great world-poets, Homer and Shakspere, fit all nations and all times. Shakspere is careless of his works, because he knows they are not his, but Some One's superior to him. In the strength of his genius, he abandons all claim to it. It is mine, 'tis yours, reader, as much as Shakspere's. This

10—2

indifference to the authorship of his works proves how really great he was.

Well has it been said, that poets are the true priests and kings of the earth; and it was no mere rhapsody that made Jean Paul Richter call Shakspere the " poetic Christ-child." In conclusion, let us remember how quietly he lived and died, known to his friends and companions by that one epithet, " gentle," and then contrast him with all the noisy, self-seeking Kaisers and Napoleons who have harried the world with misery and desolation. The thunder and the lightning attract all men's ears and eyes, but the gentle rain and the calm sunshine alone profit the earth.

Remains of Shakspere's House at New Place

A GLOSSARY OF WORDS

STILL USED IN WARWICKSHIRE

TO BE FOUND IN SHAKSPERE.

As I before stated, I by no means wish to say that the following words are to be found nowhere but in Shakspere and Warwickshire. Some, though, undoubtedly are provincialisms. And we must remember the fact, how very strongly different dialects are marked in England, and the wide difference there is, not only in the meaning, but in the pronunciation of the same words, in Dorsetshire, where the Saxon element is most marked, and in the eastern and midland counties, where the Anglian is more prominent. Thus, in the *Venus and Adonis*, Shakspere rhymes "juice" as if spelt "joyce," a thoroughly midland pronunciation of the word:—

> Ill-natured, crooked, churlish, harsh in voice,
> O'erworn, despised, rheumatic, and cold,
> Thick-sighted, barren, lean, and lacking juice.

And again, in the very next stanza, as Dr. Farmer also remarked,

" ear " is rhymed. as it is to this day pronounced in Warwickshire, as if it were " air : " —

> Bid me discourse, I will enchant thine ear,
>   Or, like a fairy, trip upon the green,
> Or, like a nymph, with long, dishevell'd hair,
>   Dance on the sands, and yet no footing seen.

I shall venture, then, to give a list of what Shaksperian words I have chiefly noticed as still in use among the peasantry of Warwickshire; premising only that the chief value is in the fact, that they are still spoken by breathing human beings, the same sort as from whose lips Shakspere learnt his mother tongue.

BATLET.—Rightly explained in the glossaries as an instrument with which washers beat their coarse clothes. I have heard women speak of their "batlet-tub." Round Stratford the former is now more commonly called " a dolly," or " a maiden." *As You Like It*, act ii. scene 4.

BAVIN.—There are several different definitions given of this word in the dictionaries; but in Warwickshire I have found it more generally to mean the scraps and scrapings of the faggot, in distinction to the faggot itself, and which so easily kindle, thus explaining the passage in the First Part of *King Henry IV.*, act iii. scene 2, " rash bavin wits soon kindled and soon burnt." Used also by Lily, in *Mother Bombie.*

BOTTLE.—" A bottle of hay," for which Bottom pines in the *Midsummer Night's Dream*, act iv. scene 1, is still a current phrase in Warwickshire, and the midland counties generally. We meet with it everywhere in common use in the proverb of " looking for a needle in a bottle of hay."

BOW.—Still means a yoke for cattle. " As the ox hath his bow, sir ; so man hath his desires."—*As You Like It*, act iii. scene 4.

BIGGEN.—A child's cap : rarely heard.

> Sleep
> Yet not so sound, and half so deeply sweet,
> As her whose brow, with homely biggen bound,
> Snores out the watch of night.

BRAVERY.—Finery. *Taming of the Shrew*, act iv. scene 3. Common among all Shakspere's contemporaries.

BRIZE.—The gadfly. Pronounced "breeze," and sometimes "bree." *Antony and Cleopatra*, act iii. scene 8. Found also in Spenser.

BROKEN TEARS.—Still used of tears, which are suddenly stopped ; though in *Troilus and Cressida*, act iv. scene 4, they seem rather to mean tears broken by sobs.

CHILDING.—Pregnant. Is very beautifully applied in the *Midsummer Night's Dream*, act ii. scene 2, to the autumn, which the common texts entirely spoil by reading "chilling." The same thought may be found expanded in the *Sonnets*,—

> The teeming autumn, big with rich increase,
> Bearing the wanton burden of the prime. *Sonnet 97.*

CLAW.—To flatter. "If a talent be a claw, look how he claws him with a talent." *Love's Labour's Lost*, act iv. scene 2.

COB-LOAF.—"A badly set up loaf," to use one country expression to explain another, with a great deal of crust upon it. "Cob," by itself, in Warwickshire, as in Oxfordshire, means a cake. And in the former county we meet with "warden-cobs," cakes in which warden pears are baked. In *Troilus and Cressida*, act ii. scene 1, Ajax calls Thersites "cob-loaf," and the allusion is to his ill-shaped head ; and in act v. scene 1, the metaphor is still carried out and explained by his being called a "crusty batch."

COMMIT.—To commit adultery. So Othello to Desdemona : "What committed, O thou public commoner ! "—*Othello*, act iv. scene 2.

CUSTOMER.—A common woman. *Othello*, act iv. scene 1; *Comedy of Errors*, act iv. scene 4.

DOUT.—A corruption of "do out :" very commonly used of putting out the candle, the extinguisher of which, as Miss Baker observes, in her *Glossary of Northamptonshire Words*, is called a "douter." To be heard also in the southern counties. Metaphorically used in *Hamlet*, act iv. scene 7.

DUP.—Formed, like the former word, from "do up." "Dup the door," or, more commonly, "sneck the door," may still be heard. *Hamlet*, act iv. scene 5.

DOXY.—As Beaumont and Fletcher say in the *Beggar's Bush*, "neither wives, maids, nor widows." Still heard, though rarely. *The Winter's Tale*, act iv. scene 2.

EANLINGS.—Young lambs just eaned, or "dropped." *The Merchant of Venice*, act i. scene 3. In *Lycidas*, Milton speaks of the "weanling herds," which means, though, the lambs that have been weaned from their dams.

FEEDERS.—Idle, good-for-nothing servants. *Timon of Athens*, act ii. scene 2. In *Antony and Cleopatra*, act iii. scene 11, we find them called "eaters," just as we now say of horses standing idle in the stable, that they are eating their heads off; or as Massinger, in *A New Way to Pay Old Debts*, act i. scene 3, says of them,—

——— born
Only to consume meat and drink, and fatten.

FORWEARIED.—Very tired. *King John*, act ii. scene 1.

FARDEL.—A faggot, or "kid," as it is more commonly called. Metaphorically used in the well-known passage in *Hamlet*, act iii. scene 1. Termed in the more southern counties a "niche."

GIB-CAT.—"I am as melancholy as a gib-cat," says Falstaff, in the First Part of *King Henry IV.*, act i. scene 2, and the proverb may not only be heard in Northamptonshire, as Miss Baker in her *Glossary* remarks, but also in Warwickshire. In our old writers a gib-cat seems to have meant a tom-cat, and the phrase probably arose because, as Linnæus observes of the animal, *miserè amat*.

HONEY-STALKS.—White clover, so called because it is so full of honey. So, in *Titus Andronicus*, act iv. scene 4, we find,—

With words more sweet, and yet more dangerous
Than baits to fish, or honey-stalks to sheep ;
When as the one is wounded with the bait,
The other rotted with delicious feed:

lines which every farmer knows to be true. I may perhaps here notice that *Titus Andronicus* contains a great number of provincial words; such as the next on the list "jet," to strut ; "shive," a slice; "urchin," a hedgehog, &c. ; which together with other internal evidence of style and language, would form a strong argument for its genuineness.

JET.—To walk, or rather strut, proudly, "like a crow in a gutter," as the common Warwickshire saying that accompanies it runs. Shakspere, however, in connection with this word in *Twelfth Night*, act ii. scene 5, uses another bird with reference to Malvolio: "Contemplation makes a rare turkey-cock of him ; how he jets under his advanced plumes."

INKLES.—A sort of common tape ; the poorest and cheapest kind being called "beggar's inkle." The phrase which Miss Baker quotes in her *Northamptonshire Glossary:* "as thick as inkle weavers," may also be heard in Warwickshire, and without the word "inkle" even in the southern and western counties. *Winter's Tale*, act iv. scene 3.

IRK.—To make uneasy. Still used impersonally: "it irks," exactly equivalent to the Latin *tædet*. *As You Like It*, act ii. scene 3.

KECK or KEX.—Used in Warwickshire and the midland counties, generally of the various species of umbelliferous plants which grow in the ditches and hedges :—

nothing teems
But hateful docks, rough thistles, kexes, burs.
Henry V., act v. scene 2.

Tennyson uses this word in *The Princess*,—

though the rough kex break
The starred mosaic.

KINDLE.—Said of animals bringing forth their young, more especially in reference to rabbits, as Rosalind uses it in *As You Like It*, act iii. scene 2. "A kindle" is sometimes used of a litter; as "trip" is in the south-western counties.

LIEF.—Soon. "I had as lief do so and so," may be heard every day in Warwickshire. See Mr. Craik's *English of Shakspere*, p. 38, and Miss Baker's *Northamptonshire Glossary*, on this word, which is current more or less throughout all the midland districts, and which I perceive is in vogue with some modern writers, but which is, of course, now a mere vulgarism. How frequently Shakspere uses it, a reference to the concordance will show. Mr. Tennyson's use of this word and its comparative "liever" in the *Idylls of the King* is very beautiful.

LATED.—benighted, belated.

> The west yet glimmers with some streaks of day,
> Now spurs the lated traveller.—*Macbeth*, act iii. scene 3.

LIFTER.—A thief. Hence, as Nares remarks, our modern phrase of "shop-lifter." *Troilus and Cressida*, act i. scene 2. Used also by Shakspere's contemporaries.

LODGE.—Still spoken of corn or any cereal, or even grass, being "laid," as the more common phrase is, by wind or rain. Thus, in *Macbeth*, act iv. scene 1, we find "though bladed corn be lodged." In Mr. Tennyson's *Idylls of the King*, we meet with the more usual expression,—

> It fell
> Like flaws in summer laying lusty corn.   *Enid.*

LOGGATS.—An old English game played in various parts of England as late as in Steevens's time. The word now, though, in Warwickshire signifies a small piece of wood, and with "logger," is sometimes used of the log or clog tied to an animal's legs to prevent its running away. *Hamlet*, act v. scene 1.

LOON.—A stupid scamp. *Macbeth*, act v. scene 3. In *Othello*, act ii. scene 3, for the sake of the rhyme, we find "lown." And so written in *Pericles*, act iv. scene 4.

MAMMET.—A doll, puppet.

> This is no world
> To play with mammets.
> The First Part of *King Henry IV.*, act ii. scene 3.

It is now, though, only used by crow-boys of their scarecrows or "malkins," which latter word is used in *Pericles*, act iv. scene 4.

MASTER.—Still used as a sort of prefix, by the lower orders, before a person's name. The same old use of the words may be found in other parts of England, but never so commonly, I think, as in Warwickshire, where "good Master Fenton," and "good Master Brook," would still be so called, if they were now alive.

MORTAL.—In *As You Like It*, act ii. scene 4, we find, "so is all nature in love, mortal in folly :" that is, to use the common country expression, mortally foolish, or very foolish. The late Mr. Singer, in his edition of Shakspere, compares it with the expression, to be heard in Warwickshire and the midland districts, of "mortal tall," mortal little."

NINE MEN'S MORRIS.—The nine men's morris board, instead of being on the turf, is now more frequently cut on the corn-bins of the stables at the Warwickshire farm-houses, and the ploughmen use white and black beans to distinguish their men ; the great object being to get three of them in a row, or, as it is called, to have a "click-clack and an open row." In order to do this, you are allowed to take up your adversary's pieces as at draughts, or else to hem them up till they cannot move. There is also a game called "three men's morris," which is much simpler.

NOUL.—A head. In the *Midsummer Night's Dream*, act iii. scene 2, Puck talks about "the ass's noul" he has fixed on Bottom's head. And the word is still so used, both of animals and men, but always implying stupidity.

PASH.—A rough head. "Thou wantest a rough pash," says Leontes to his little son, in the *Winter's Tale*, act i. scene 2. I have sometimes heard the compound expression, "a pash-head," used.

PATCH.—A fool, simpleton. "A crew of patches," *The Midsummer Night's Dream*, act iii. scene 2. Bottom, in his zeal, becomes tautological, when he says, in the same play, act iv. scene 1, "Man is but a patched fool." And the adjective "patched" still means foolish.

PICKTHANKS.—Tale-bearers. The First Part of *King Henry IV.*, act iii. scene 2. During the rejoicings at Stratford on the conclusion of the Crimean war, I heard a peasant, saying of the public tea-meeting, &c., held in the High Street, "There will be pickthanking work to-morrow ;" that is, tale-bearing, gossiping, not unmixed with grumbling.

PUN.—To pound. *Troilus and Cressida*, act ii. scene 1. Warwickshire country people nearly always speak of "punning fat." Nares appositely quotes Dr. Johnson as an authority for the use of the word in the midland counties.

QUAT.—A small pimple, pustule, boil. Metaphorically used in *Othello*, act v. scene 1. Used also in the southern counties.

RACE.—" A race of ginger," that is, a stick of ginger. *The Winter's Tale*, act iv. scene 2.

RAVIN.—To devour voraciously. *Measure for Measure*, act i. scene 3.

RID.—To destroy. "The red plague rid you," *The Tempest*, act i. scene 2.

SAGG.—To tire, to sink down. A Warwickshire labourer will still speak of being "sagged," and of a "sagging job," that is, a tiring, fatiguing job. Applied metaphorically in *Macbeth*, act v. scene 3. Miss Baker very well explains this word in her *Glossary of Northamptonshire Words*.

SALT.—In *Antony and Cleopatra*, act ii. scene 1, we meet with the singular expression of "salt Cleopatra," a phrase which none of the commentators have ventured to explain. It is still used of common women.

SHIVE.—A slice. We still hear of " cutting a shive ;" and the proverb in *Titus Andronicus*, act ii. scene 1, " It is easy to steal a shive of a cut loaf," is still common in the midland and northern counties.

SHOG.—To jog off, make off. So Nym, in *Henry V.*, act ii. scene 3, says, " Shall we shog off ? "

SHOVEL-BOARD.—*The Merry Wives of Windsor*, act i. scene 1. A portion of the table in some of the Warwickshire public-houses is still marked out as the shovel-board, upon which a coin is jerked with the open hand to a given mark, the winner being the person who jerks it the nearest. A tradition exists in Stratford that Shakspere used to play shovel-board at the Falcon.

SQUASH.—An unripe pea-pod. So Leontes, in the *Winter's Tale*, act i. scene 2, calls his son " this kernel, this squash ;" and Bully Bottom, in the *Midsummer Night's Dream*, act iii, scene 1, christens Fairy Peablossom's mother " Mistress Squash."

Statute-caps.—Woollen caps, compelled to be worn by an Act in 1571, for the encouragement of the woollen trade. The name still lingers in some parts of the county, though not applied to woollen caps in particular. *Love's Labour's Lost,* act v. scene 2.

Tills.—The shafts of a waggon. "An you draw backward, we'll put you i' the tills." *Troilus and Cressida,* act iii. scene 2. And in the *Merchant of Venice* we meet with "Dobbin, the phill-horse;" a phrase which may be still heard.

Urchin.—A hedgehog. In the *Venus and Adonis* Shakspere calls the boar "urchin snouted," that is, with a nose like a hedgehog. The common notes on the passage say, "urchin, that is, a sea-porcupine." But the word is the common term in Warwickshire and the midland districts for a hedgehog, which is so called in old works on natural history. *Titus Andronicus,* act ii. scene 3.

Wench.—A young maid. Still used in its primitive sense as a term of endearment throughout the midland districts, as we find it in the old version of the Scriptures. "A chap and his wench," merely signifies a young fellow and his sweetheart. So Petruchio, in the *Taming of the Shrew,* act v. scene 2, when all has been made pleasant, says, "Why there's a wench, come on and kiss me, Kate." Every one will remember how Oliver Cromwell pathetically speaks of his children as "my two little wenches," Carlyle's *Life of Cromwell,* Supplement, p. 143.

Whip-stock.—A carter's whip-handle. "Malvolio's nose is no whip-stock," *Twelfth Night,* act ii. scene 3.*

---

* Since this Glossary was made, I have read *Clerical Scenes,* and *Adam Bede,* and the *Mill on the Floss,* written by one who knows Warwickshire well, and I could not help being struck with many of the provincialisms of the different characters; how, for instance, in Janet's Repentance, p. 75, Mrs. Lowme is described by Mrs. Phipps as "yellow as any crow-flower;" and how again, in the *Mill on the Floss,* vol. ii. p. 278, we find the same expression; how, too, in *Adam Bede,* vol. i. p. 79, Joshua Rann, the parish clerk, says, he has lived in the village "man and boy sixty years come St. Thomas;" how, also, in Mr. Gilfil's *Love Story*

Mr. Bellamy speaks of Sir Christopher, as " a gentleman born ; " how, in the *Mill on the Floss*, Mr. Tulliver affectingly calls Maggie " his little wench," and how we find the words " lief," and " master " constantly used.

All these are Warwickshire expressions, and, as we have seen, used by Shakspere; and it is striking, after the lapse of nearly three hundred years, to find them once more reproduced in literature.

One word more: I feel certain that many obscure passages, both in Shakspere and all our Elizabethan dramatists, might be cleared up, if a more constant reference were made to our provincialisms.

Cadent

—— in honore vocabula :

And a word, which two or three centuries ago was perfectly intelligible and in current use, is now quite obsolete, except as a provincialism, spoken only here and there by uneducated country people.

Autograph

INDEX.

All's Well that Ends Well, 95.

Alveston, village of, 46 ; pastures, 46.

Andronicus, Titus, 153, 157.

Angelo, Michael, 49.

Apple-John, mentioned by Shakspere, 97, 98.

Aquilegia vulgaris, 60.

Arden, forest of, in Warwickshire, 53, 54.

Ardens, family of; the name of Shakspere's mother, 64.

As You Like It, 54, 94, 109, 128, 145, 150, 153, 155.

Ashbies, farm of, near Wimpcote, belonged to Shakspere's father, 38, 68.

Astrology, in Shakspere's day, 139.

Athens, Timon of, 114, 129, 152.

Aubrey, his account of Shakspere, 39, 77.

Autolycus, song of, 101 (*footnote*), 106.

Avon, the, 21, 45, 75.

Baker, Miss, 60, 109, 113, 151, 152, 153.

Batlet, meaning of, 150.

Barson, village of, mentioned by Shakspere, 79.

Beaumont, 133, 146.

Bede, Adam, 157.

Bell, Mr. Robert, 60.

Bidford, 74, 89.

Biggen, a, 151.

Binton Hill, 68, 91.

Biographies, the worthlessness of most, 3.

Bishopton, 59, 98.

Bitter-sweet, the, mentioned in *Romeo and Juliet*, 97.

Boltered, blood-, meaning of, in *Macbeth*, 113.

Bombie, Mother, 150.

Boscobel Tracts, the, 89 (*footnote*).

Bottle, a, in Shakspere, 150.

Bow, meaning of, 150.

Brake, the weir, near Stratford, 80.

Bravery, still used for finery in Warwickshire, 151.

Bredon Hill, 68.

Brize, the meaning of, 151.

Broken tears, meaning of, 151.

Broom, "beggarly," 90.

Burton Heath, village of, mentioned in the *Taming of the Shrew*, 79.

Bush, the Beggar's, 152.

Bushes, the Snitterfield, 64.

Cade, Jack, 125.

Caps, Statute, 157.

Carlyle, Mr., 121.

Cat, Gib-, 152.

Chamberlain's accounts of Stratford, 17 (*footnote*), 35, 36.

Chancel of Stratford Parish Church, 26.

Chapel of the Guild at Stratford, 17 ; used as a schoolroom, 29, 30.

Charlecote Park, 43.

Charles II., King, 67, 88.

Childhood, how connected with poetry, 6 ; Shakspere's love of, 125.
Childing, the meaning of, in the *Midsummer Night's Dream*, 151.
Church, Luddington, 82; Stratford Parish, 20; Weston, 92.
Cider, Philips' poem of, 98.
Claw, meaning of, 151.
Cleeve, village of, 97.
Clopton,' Sir Hugh, 31; house, 63; lane 16, 68.
Coat, the leather-, 96.
Cob-loaf, meaning of, 151.
Cockaim, Sir Aston, 78; poems of, 76 (*footnote*).
Coleridge, on the effects of scenery, 6.
College of Stratford, 28.
Collier, Mr., his researches, 4, 5, 144; folio of, 76.
Combe, John, 25.
Comedy of Errors, 33, 151.
Commit, meaning of, 151.
Coriolanus, 37, 126, 137.
Corporation books of Stratford, 38.
Cottage, Anne Hathaway's, 71.
Cotsall Hills, the, 50, 78.
Crab-John, 98; Shakspere's crab-tree, 86, 90; *the Legend of*, by C. F. Green, 91 (*footnote*).
Cressida, Troilus and, 80, 113, 126, 156.
Crow-flowers, meaning of, in Shakspere, 61, 157.
Crow-toe, in Milton, 62.
Culver-keys, meaning of, 63.
Customer, meaning of, 151.

Dante, 22, 49, 120.
Dannce of Death, the 30 (*footnote*).
Davies, Rev. R., MS. of, 51 (*footnote*).
Deck, meaning of, in Warwickshire, 105.
Dill-cup, meaning of, 62.
Dingles, the, near Stratford, 59.
Dont, to, meaning of, 151.
Doxy, meaning of, 152.
Drayton, 5, 8 (*footnote*), 53.

Dugdale, *History of Warwickshire* by, 31, 52 (*footnote*).
Dup, to, meaning of, 152.

Eanlings, meaning of, 152.
Ear, pronounced air, by Shakspere, 150.
Eaters, meaning of, 152.
Edgehill, battle of, 92.
Eglantine, the sweet-briar of Shakspere, 129.
" Elm, one," the, at Stratford, 59, 68.
Epigram on Malone, 24 (*footnote*).
Epitaph on Shakspere, 21 ; on Shakspere's daughter, Susannah Hall, 22; on John Combe, 26 (*footnote*).
Errors, Comedy of, 109, 151.
Eversham, vale of, 90.
Exhall, " dodging," 91.

Fairy Queen, the, 22.
Falcon Inn, the, at Stratford, 14, 18 (*footnote*); at Bidford, 77 (*footnote*), 89.
Falstaff, 124.
Fardel, meaning of, 152.
Farm, the Cherry Orchard, 76 ; Hungry Arbour, 91.
Feeders, meaning of, 152.
Fingers, King's, in *Hamlet*, 61 (*footnote*) ; dead men's, 61 (*footnote*).
Fisher, Clement, of Wincot, 76.
Flowers, their value, 10 ; names of, true poetry, 63 ; Shakspere's love of, 9, 10.
Forwearied, meaning of, 152.
Fulbrook Park, 52.

Gastrel, Rev. Francis, 30.
Gib-cat, meaning of, 152.
Goethe, his account of himself, 22.
Golding, on the word " rother," 32 (*footnote*).
Grace, herb of, 100.
Grafton, " hungry," 91.
Grammar School, the, of Stratford, 17, 29.
Great men, how they should be regarded, 2.

"Great House," the, at Stratford, 17.
Groat's Worth of Wit, Greene's, 111.
Guild Hall, the, at Stratford, 17.
Gull, meaning of, in Shakspere and Warwickshire, 114.

Hall, the, of the Stratford Guild, 29.
Hall, Dr., 22.
Halliwell, accuracy of, 37 (*footnote*), 145 (*footnote*) ; life of Shakspere by, 15 (*footnote*) ; researches, of, 4, 5.
Hamlet, 111, 134, 152, 154.
Hare-hunting, described by Shakspere, 47, 48.
Harvest-homes, Warwickshire, 99.
Hathaway, Anne, 71.
Hatton Rock, near Charlecote, 55.
Henley Street, 14, 16.
Henry IV., First Part of, 97, 112, 150, 152, 154, 155 ; *Second Part of*, 50, 76, 78, 79, 96, 107, 109, 113.
Henry V., 109, 111, 156.
Henry VI., Second Part of, 125 ; *Third Part of*, 105.
Herb-o'-grace, 100.
Hero-worship, its value, 5, 16.
Herbert, Lord, of Cherbury, 10.
Hill, Binton, 68, 91 ; Cross of the, 75 ; Meon, 68 ; Rhcon, 56.
Hillborough, "haunted," 84, 90.
Holditch, 83.
Honey-stalks, meaning of, in *Titus Andronicus*, 152.
Humour, definition of, 124.
Huntington, Robert Earl of, 101 (*footnote*).

Icknield Street, 89.
Idylls of the King, 154.
Ingon Meadow Farm, 37, 64.
Inkle, meaning of, 153.
Irk, use of, in Warwickshire, 153.

Jet, to, meaning of, 153.
John-apple, mentioned by Shakspere, 97.

John, King, 132, 134.
Johnson, Gerard, 24 ; Dr., on Shakspere, 104, 112.
Jonson, Ben, 2, 29.
Juice, pronounced " joyce " by Shakspere, 149.
Juliet, Romeo and, 97, 112.

Keck or Kex, 153.
Ket, Francis, 138.
Keys, culver,—meaning of, 63.
Kindle, meaning of, 153.
King, Idylls of the, 154.
King's fingers, meaning of, 61 (*footnote*).
King's Lane, the, near Stratford, 67.
Knight, Charles, 54, 74.

Lane, Jane, 67.
Lated, use of, in Warwickshire, 154.
Lear, King, 124, 127.
Leather-coat, the, mentioned by Shakspere, 96.
Lief, use of, in Warwickshire, 153,158.
Life, troubles of, 11, 85.
Lifter, meaning of, 154.
Littleton, village of, 97.
Lodge, to, meaning of, 154.
Loggats, meaning of, 154.
Long-purples, meaning of, in *Hamlet*, 60, 105.
Loon, meaning of, 154.
Love's Labour's Lost, 62, 95.
Love-in-idleness, still the Warwickshire name for the pansy, as in Shakspere, 62.
Luce, the old name of a pike, 51.
Lucy, lines on Sir Thomas, 44 (*footnote*).
Luddington, village of, where Shakspere was married, 82.

Macbeth, 107, 113.
Malone, 24; epigram on, 24 (*footnote*).
Malkin, the meaning of, 154.
Malt, dearth of, in Stratford in 1598, 40.
Malta, the Jew of, 138.

162 INDEX.

Mammet, meaning of, 154.
Marlowe, 145.
Marston, "dancing," 88.
Master, use of, in Warwickshire, 155, 158.
Meadows, the, round Stratford, 7, 8.
Men, great, lives of unknown, 3.
Meon Hill, 68.
Merry Wives of Windsor, the, 49, 78.
Midsummer Night's Dream, the, 47, 77, 80, 81, 82, 95, 145, 150, 155, 157; date of, 85; tradition about, 80.
Mill, Grange, 83.
Milton, 10, 22, 117.
Morality, its full signification, 119.
Morris, nine men's, 105, 155.
Mortal, meaning of, 155.
Mountains, modern love of, 10 (*footnote*).
Mulberry-tree, Shakspere's, 30.
Munday, Antony, 101 (*footnote*).

New Place, 17, 30; Queen Henrietta Maria at, 30; bought by Shakspere, 39.
Nibelungen Lied, unknown author of the, 3.
Niche, meaning of, 152.
Night, Twelfth, 137.
Nothing, Much Ado about, 77, 107, 108, 109.
Northamptonshire Words, Glossary of, by Miss Baker, 60 (*footnote*), 109, 151, 152, 156.
Noul, meaning of, 155.
Novalis, upon Shakspere, 130.

Oak, Herne's, 69.
Old, meaning of, in Shakspere and the Elizabethan dramatists, 107.
Oldys MS., the, 78.
Ophelia, songs of, 99.
Orchard, Cherry, the, 76.
Othello, 151, 154, 156.

Paintings, in the Chapel of the Guild at Stratford, 30.
Paradise Lost, 49.

Pash, meaning of, 155.
Patch, meaning of, 155.
Patriotism, Shakspere's, 132.
Pear, warden-, mentioned by Shakspere, 96.
Pebworth, "piping," 89.
Pedlars' songs, from Shakspere and Munday, 101 (*footnote*).
Perkes, Clement, 77.
Pickthanks, meaning of, 155.
Plato, 122, 123, 142.
Poet, the reflex of his time, 18, 19, 141.
Poets, love of, for flowers, 9, 10.
Poetry, definition of, 44; what it is, 74.
Polyolbion, Drayton's, 8 (*footnote*).
Powles, Church of, 30 (*footnote*).
Princess, the, 153.
Prick-eared, meaning of, 111.
Protestantism, true meaning of, as seen in Shakspere, 140.
Proverbs, in Shakspere, 109 (*footnote*).
Provincialisms of Shakspere, 103, 149.
Pun, to, meaning of, 156.
Puritans, the, in Shakspere's day, 139.
Purples, long, what they are in *Hamlet*, 60, 105.

Quat, a, meaning of, 156.
Quiney, Richard, letter from, to Shakspere, 41.
Quoth, use of the word in Shakspere and Warwickshire, 112.

Race, meaning of, 156.
Radbrook, village of, 81.
Ravin, meaning of, 156.
Register, parish, Luddington, 82; Snitterfield, 64; Stratford, 23; Welford, 83; Weston, 76.
Repository, the Shaksperian, 83 (*footnote*).
Rheon Hill, 56.
Richter, Jean Paul, 5, 44; on Shakspere, 147.

Roads, summer, meaning of, 108.
Rock, Hatton, 55.
Rother Street, in Stratford, 32.
Rother, explanation of, as used by Shakspere, 32 (*footnote*).

Sagg, to, meaning of, 156.
Salt, meaning of, 156.
Scenery, local, its effects on a poet, 6 ; modern love for, 10 (*footnote*).
Schlegel on Shakspere's Sonnets, 145.
Shakspère, John : his varying circumstances, 36, 37 ; his death, 39.
Shakspere, William: his life, a collection of fines and leases, 4 ; chief excellence, 11, 12 ; his good fortune in his birthplace, 5, 6 ; where buried, 21, 22 ; love for flowers, 10, 63, 65, 128 ; deeply religious tone of mind, 25, 26, 27, 137 ; his sonnets, 3, 27, 145 ; his humour, 124, 125 ; his love for nature, 65, 127, 128 ; his views of life, how affected by the age in which he lived, 141, 142 ; his wide catholic spirit, 137 ; his patriotism, 132 ; the true artist, 133 ; his Protestantism, 140 ; his indifference about his works a sign of his true greatness, 146.
Shaksperian Repository, the, 83 (*footnote*).
Sheep, pronunciation of, in Shakspere, 33.
Shive, meaning of, 156.
Shog, meaning of, 156.
Shottery, village of, where Anne Hathaway lived, 70.
Shovel-board, still used in Warwickshire, 105, 156.
Shrew, Taming of the, 107, 109.
Singer, Mr., the late, 32, 155.
Skelton, 87.
Slobberly, meaning of, 109.
Snitterfield, 64 ; where Shakspere's

father held some property, 64 ; Bushes, 65.
Sonnets, the, of Shakspere, 3, 27, 145.
Spenser, 10, 22.
Squash, meaning of, 156.
Stour, river, 81.
Straight, meaning of, in *Hamlet* 111.1.
Stratford-upon-Avon, 12 ; meadows round, 7, 8 ; derivation of Stratford, 14 ; in the sixteenth century, 16, 17 ; *Wheler's History of,* 18 (*footnote*) ; alehouses in Stratford in Shakspere's time, 18 (*footnote*) ; parish church of, 20 ; college of, 28 ; grammar school, 29 ; Chamberlain's accounts of, 17 (*footnote*), 35, 36.
Statute-caps, the name still preserved in Warwickshire, 157.
Sweeting, bitter-, mentioned by Shakspere, 97.

Taming of the Shrew, the, popular tradition about, 77 (*footnote*), 78, 107.
Tempest, the, 104, 109.
Tills, meaning of, 157.
Tomes, manor-house of the, 88 ; Mr. R. F. Tomes, 103 (*footnote*).
Tooth, pugging-, explanation of, in the *Winter's Tale,* 106.
Traditions, their value, 26, 27.

Ulrici, on Shakspere, 74, 141.
Urchin, meaning of, 157.
Utopia, Gonzalo's, 125.

Venice, Merchant of, the, 107, 108, 134, 152, 157.
Venus and Adonis, 47, 48, 127, 149, 160.
Vicarage, Weston, 84.
Virgil, description of the willow by, 7 (*footnote*).

Ward, Rev. John, 87.
Warden pear, 96 ; cob, 96.

Warwickshire, Drayton's description of, 8 (*footnote*); Dugdale's, 31, 52 (*footnote*); provincialisms, 103, 149; harvest-homes, 99; orchards, 96.

Weanlings, meaning of, 152.

Welcombe, 59.

Welford, village of, 82; extract from the parish register of, 83.

Weir-brake, the, 80.

Weston Sands, 82, 96.

Wench, used still in its primitive signification in the midland districts, 157, 158.

Wheler, *History of Stratford*, by, 18 (*footnote*); collection of Shaksperian papers by, 60 (*footnote*).

Whipstock, meaning of, 157.

Wimpcote, or Wilmecote, where Shakspere's mother lived, 68.

Wincot, village of, mentioned in the *Taming of the Shrew*, 76.

Windsor, Merry Wives of, 49, 78.

Winter's Tale, the, 65, 96, 99, 101, 126, 152, 153, 155, 156.

Wit, Groat's Worth of, 111.

Witches, how held in Shakspere's day, 139.

Witch, mankind, meaning of, 104.

Wixford, "papist," 90.

Women, Shakspere's, 121.

Wordsworth, 118, 131.

Worcester, battle of, 88.

www.ingramcontent.com/pod-product-compliance
Lightning Source LLC
Chambersburg PA
CBHW032227080426
42735CB00008B/751